Sharecropper's Son

to

T.B.:
A fellow Ph.D.;
I hope you enjoy this
little book;
Bert Hayes
21 Jan '09

Memories and Interpretations by Bert Hayes Ph.D

white sidewall balloon tires and appurtenances and boasted Bendix coaster brakes. Not having these things taught me how much I can do without and still be happy. "What did you get for Christmas?" was not a popular question in the local schools in January.

I know how solid we were in those days. America had a high percentage of subsistence population who, for the most part, were landowners. Other subsistence families on the land were sharecroppers and tenants. Regionally there was variation in the picture when we consider the Mississippi Delta, the Tennessee Valley of Alabama, the Alabama Black Belt, the Georgia/South Carolina plains, etc. The Piedmont in all the states was peculiar to itself. My parents in the Georgia Piedmont were "Piedmont Proletariats" (not to be confused with Karl Marx's Theory) with so many children they could never produce an excess of capital to buy land.

Now comes the scary part. Since the Grand Depression, our nation's urban (now includes suburban and penurban) population has increased to about ninety-five percent of the total. This includes most of the previous subsistence agricultural population and small semi-agricultural operators who have joined the non-agricultural ranks. I imagine the consequences today when ninety-five percent of the population depends on the elite minority (corporate agriculture and support groups) for food and other commodities. Admittedly, high tech and the sciences enable the elite minority to produce for the ninety-five

percent but... high tech and science keep the general population in a state of retraining and migratory flux so the seeming gains in employment do not employ the perpetually unemployed. This encourages the planned obsolescence of goods and services to keep the cash flow going and reduces the quality of goods and services. We end up with jiggle and junk. This system is very impressive in "innovations" but remains a "wake-up call" to those of us from the Depression Era. "Something jus' isn't right" sez we. Our modern safeguards do include federally insured bank deposits and social security benefits but that's about the only difference.

Having said that about the shaky "devolutionary" process going on, I must support the notion that the current lack of moral fiber in the younger generation in "non sua culpa" (is not their fault). They have not been shocked and awed, as we were by the times and events that "try men's souls." I suspect that the good, the conservative and the patriotic are still in the majority yet we are passive and do not have the aggressiveness of the vocal minority who are undermining and sapping our walls of defense or our "Seyag le Torah" as the Rabbis say. We are guilty of not suppressing the "rising expectation" philosophy which concludes that "not only are matters good, but they're going to get better" and any ordinary decline of the economy is license to blame the government.

The Roaring, Flapping Twenties are being outdone by a minority whose heroes are rock stars, movie

stars, urban cowboys, TV personalities, overpaid athletes, and immoral politicians who are even a smaller population with an inordinate amount of influence on the vocal, demonstrative minority. These obscure the impending reality of a nation terribly in debt, targeted by evil forces around the world bent on destroying us and they obscure also the arduous route we must take to correct it. Some perceive life as a smorgasbord and not a bill of fare, a smorgasbord from which they can choose their likes and leave the dislikes.

The Good Book says that there is a season for everything including sadness and happiness yet in this dualism of everything, the noisy minority elects to accept only the enjoyable, even emphasizing "rights" to the total neglect of responsibility. Our soldiers are dying to protect our freedom, not our frivolity. In the Depression, we had fun when we could via the most ingenious and inexpensive ways but we had more concern about our armed forces and the support personnel.

Listen, my children, I may be a dinosaur who drives his own car and flies his own plane and has modest training in the arts and sciences, yet I am not attacking right vs. wrong. I'm just saying that it's a question of superior vs. inferior. I'm attacking inferior language, philosophy, values and attitudes: I'm not judging morality or frivolity.

I must advise you that I'm not spouting "Old Fogeyism" related to my growing senility. I am

speaking from a timeless universalism that differentiates permanency from transitoriness and classical from popular. Ronald Reagan was challenged at a university (University of Kansas, I think) by a student who suggested that Mr. Reagan simply rejected change. The student got a quietening broadside "Young man, I have seen more changes in my lifetime than you will ever see." He enumerated the changes in science and technology and he further explained that changes must be viewed in the static context and "change for change sake" is not a solution. "Change for change sake," reminds me of our dear friend J. W. of the 101st Airborne who saw action in Vietnam. In his civilian life, he still toted around his old globe-trotting luggage. While checking into luxury hotel in the U. S. some rude, nattily dressed snob guest confronted J. W. with, "Excuse me, you're not checking in with 'those' bags are you?" J. W. turned quietly and replied "Sir, these bags have been to places of which you may only dream." Go, J. W., you've always said the right thing at the right time.

If, when reading this little book, you find no errors in orthography, morphology, syntax, grammar, composition, facts, figures and historical memory, you're not very perceptive. (Applicable to me and Nikita Krushev is the admonition "Never educate a peasant.") Neither should you expect the usual testimonies of the Depression and World War II generation. There are excellent fictions (based on

good facts) from these eras and well-worth reading. I'm not attempting to view these great periods of history from the standpoint of big landowners (*lantifundistas*), tycoons, white collar drifters, unemployment, Hollywood placebos, Jazz and Blues, etc. Sure, I remember hunger, thirst, hog killing, watermelon thumping, blackberry picking, pokeberry sallat, toothache, diarrhea from poor food, holes in my britches, humid summers, shivering winters, long distances to walk, and all of the above compounded. I participated in the bedrock South and realize that this was true reality, solid and perpetual. My real regret was not being able to participate in the advance of science and technology. Now I assume the posture of kneeling in admiration at their greatness while promoting my own philosophy inherited from the good folks of the Georgia Piedmont.

ROYSTON

In worldly values, Royston ranked little to nothing, therefore Royston offered the best potential for the growth and usefulness of its citizens. Read the words of John H. Hall carefully:

A superficial glance at the world at large - the various zones, climates, races... inclines the casual observer to the opinion that there is great inequality in distribution of endowments and environments. But a closer view of places, persons and preferment will reveal the fact that advantages as to locality have their counter-balancing disadvantage, and superior endowment is offset by corresponding indolence - or disregard of the greater responsibility attached. So, we find that where "nature" has done most for man, he does least in the way of utilizing her munificent gifts - and 'tis so in the realm of intellect as well. (Seed Thoughts and alliterative Aphorisms, 1924, p. 68.)

"Great oaks from little acorns grow."

At approximately thirty-four degrees - twenty minutes Latitude North and eighty-three degrees - eight minutes longitude West, in effect, about 20 miles from South Carolina and about 60 miles from North Carolina, Royston lies on a modest plateau in the Georgia Piedmont. I sensed the orientation as a child and my adult training in geography and aviation has given me the technical confirmation. I'm about to

present the matrix and milieu of a remarkable area that does more than hold the earth together at latitude/longitude and "down to China." I remember several Roystonians who had a romantic view of the area and I'm indebted to them for their inspiration. My third grade teacher, Ms. Lee, described the length and importance of U. S. Highway 29, which ran from "foreign" places such as the State of Maine to Pensacola, Florida, and Ms. Ginn, my fourth grade teacher, who jump-started me into the awesome world of geography. I matured geographically rapidly thereafter because the Japanese bombed Pearl Harbor and Montgomery and Rommel chased each other back and forth between Tabruq and Alamein in the North African desert. Other teachers and neighbors will appear in this volume as my mind re-focuses.

Now back to the Royston plateau and the environs... There will always be the critics who refuse to acknowledge the grandeur of the Georgia Piedmont so let me throw a little cold water on their psyches. I've been around the world, studied the Dead Sea (1280 feet below sea level), traveled to Tibet and camped at 16,000 feet (above sea level), looked through my binoculars at awesome Mt. Everest and the Himalayan peaks, yet Royston and the Georgia Piedmont still hold a mystique for me that captivated my childhood and stir my nostalgia today. You strangers to the region should travel there and follow my directions and you'll discover and feel more than the local population does.

The aforementioned plateau begins at Toccoa, Georgia and spreads southwards, crowned by Georgia Highway 17, which runs south to Central Georgia. Northwards is Toccoa Creek, which sheds the water from Toccoa Falls (186' high) and contributes to Tugaloo River (now the backwater of the great Savannah River Dam at Hartwell, Georgia). From Toccoa southwards, the plateau is several miles wide and from seven to nine hundred feet above sea level. Near Royston, there are two elevations of nearly 1300', which serve as lookouts over the Georgia Piedmont. The lookout nearest Royston promotes a view north to conical Curahee Mountain and the Blue Ridge Range which flaunts its snow in winter. On your visit to Royston, turn south on the road by the Ty Cobb hospital and it's only a mile to the high point. Maybe you local folks can find this lookout point and appreciate it.

The plateau provides the basic watershed creeks, which gain volume and speed on the east to the Savannah River and on the west to the Broad River, which becomes the Big Sandy Broad. In my observation, the watershed to the west is more precipitous. Proceed west on Hwy. 29 through Franklin Springs and observe that Highway 29 begins to lose elevation rapidly and crosses the Broad River Bridge en route to Athens south-southwest of Royston. Both the plateau and the watershed creeks figure prominently in the history and economy of the post Civil War Era (Royston began about 1880).

Briefly, I'll anticipate your questions by indication that the creeks provided waterpower for corn mills and the springs provided household water. Occasionally springs (such as Franklin Springs) were spas, boasting mineral, sulphur and pure water in close proximity to one another. Other springs, such as Poplar Springs near Canon, were religious campgrounds for both Sunday and weekly meeting.

Of course, some may dispute my "plateau" notion of Royston and the environs, especially people acquainted with more identifiable plateaus such as "Sand Mountain" plateau between Chattanooga, TN and Cullman, AL. "Sand Mountain" averages about twenty miles wide and over a hundred miles long with only occasional minor breaks. The elevations are about 900' but the sheds are simply drop-offs to the Tennessee River on the West and Valley Head to Birmingham on the East. The traveler goes up to Sand Mountain, and then downward no matter which direction he travels. Sand Mountain has the heralded reputation of turning the mighty Tennessee River back toward the northwest and to the Ohio River. Then, of course, there are the great mesas in the west, etc.

Royston officially began about 1880 when W. A. Royston bought some land and put up some buildings at the very appropriate flat place, which now is an intersection of Hwy. 29 and Hwy. 17. Of course, the beginning was neither accidental nor miraculous. A movement had been going on since the end of the Civil War to produce more cotton to recover the

market from Egypt (which had begun to supply England) and also to meet the growing demands of U. S. textile manufacturing. Cotton had been grown from Atlanta to Savannah in less than adequate quantities before the war but with General Sherman's "urban renewal program" and the march to the sea, cotton production had to be regained and re-engineered.

Vertical Production (more per acre etc.) was unheard of. Horizontal Production (more acres) was the general practice so cotton production spread in many directions in Georgia - north, east, south and west. "North" was a problem because the Pine Barrens that bordered Sherman's March to the sea were a natural barrier to horizontal expansion. So... leapfrog the barrens and develop the Georgia Piedmont. Some land on the plateau had already opened to row crops or "patch" farming but once the craze started, forests were cleared to provide "new ground" for planting row crops. One must admit that none lacked for firewood in the 1870s, '80s and '90s, when "new ground" was being opened up. Moreover, railroad ties were needed for the tracks, which now ran directly through Royston just off the main intersection. (A separate book could be written about the interesting railway stations along the way.)

"New ground" had only limited space and nutrient value. The humus and topsoil were thin in the Piedmont and no sooner had the stumps decayed or were pulled for more efficient use of teams and plows, than a regional call came for imported fertilizer.

Now Grandpa and Papa had earned some money splitting and adzing logs for crossties and growing grains and vegetables for home consumption but growing cotton with commercial fertilizer was inevitable. The rails began to import "guano" ("bird dung") from Chile and Peru, thus bringing about "Catch - 22" and the revolving door. Even before the coming of the boll weevil, the farmer realized little profit from cotton and some, unable to own their own land, were at the mercy of the landlords. Quips about sharecropping were "the landlord shares with his family, not the cropper" and little dialogues emerged:

"Hey neighbor, where ya' goin' with that fertilizer?"
"I'm gonna to plant cotton!"
"Whatcha gonna do with the cotton?"
"I'm gonna sell it to pay for the fertilizer!"

Nevertheless, the process went on and the sharecropper pretended to be earning a living and surviving.

One must understand (at least I believe it) that the generation of the 1880s and the turn of the century were a unique crowd. They seemed to have gotten more out of the soil and more out of life than those who followed by experiencing the depressions, the frivolous Twenties and the subsequent collapse of the economy. Royston had something to offer in those days. There was a robust "joy of living," basic morality and belief in divine providence and great

14

optimism for the future. There had been a national "depression" in the 1890s, which led to the famous Granger Movement, but in my studies, I feel that Royston was not greatly affected. My family did move briefly to South Carolina to farm with the Manleys yet the recovery was soon forthcoming.

Ty Cobb, born in 1887, inherited the vigor of the age and also a classical education. I am greatly impressed by the continuation of Latin in the nomenclature. First names such as Albertus, Claudius, Tyrus, Theodus, etc. appeared on the farm and villages. Papa and Mama had three years of formal schooling and could communicate with college graduates with comparative ease. Ty Cobb was better educated in the classics than the sportscasters who typed him as a "demon of the diamond" and Ty could explain his aggressiveness by quoting Hamlet and Pelonius. Ty's father, Hershel, was attracted by the vigor and opportunities of Royston and brought his educator skills there.

I would have enjoyed Old Royston, "Horse and Buggy" Royston in effect while the soil had nutrition, while there were many heroes and few to no celebrities. I feel that Royston is one fine example of a glorious past and a less glorious present. The "good old days" in many areas were not "good." My children, take these words, visit Royston, screen out the artificial modernity and live in the past for a moment in time.

Yes, the creeks ran into the rivers and the rivers

into the sea and the sea is not full. Cromer's Mill Creek, Parham Mill Creek and Mason's Mill Creek ground the maize and sometimes graham flour from wheat to nourish a vital generation. (Incidentally, a proper name plus "Mill" identifies a creek; a proper name plus "Ferry" identifies a river). There were only latches with pull strings on the outside doors. Epidemics were not rampant until returning soldiers from the First War in Europe brought back the flu.

The reason I can write with authority about the "old" Royston (really "young" in the 1800s) is that I lived it, albeit I lived a double life. Papa was born in 1880 and I was born in 1931, the eleventh of twelve sharecropping youngsters. We were rural dwellers with few to no amenities. We had no plumbing, no electricity, no power tools, no automobile and no tractor in fact, nothing that could be described as modern.

The above was one life; at school was another life beginning with the third grade. The early schools boasted only a metal coal heater and an outdoor privy. Royston had central heat with radiators and indoor toilets! My home atmosphere, training and experience were the dominant force. I listened to my papa's stories and experiences, which were based on the energy and solidarities of the 1800s. His life changed very little if one can factor in twelve children as immutable! Subsistence was his philosophy and destiny as a "patch" farmer, the cash crop in the early years being railroad ties and middle years being

Georgia. Roger and Lou drew a blank on Royston so I kidded Lou "Royston is the hometown of Ty Cobb, a baseball player." Lou was at the time chasing Ty's stolen base record. Lou managed a discrete smile while Roger chuckled audibly.

Now that event was over twenty years ago, but often I have thought about writing so that my grand and great-grandchildren will know more about their origins and connections. Employment, caring for older siblings and helping rear and educate my children have kept me from writing but certainly not from thinking. I have felt obligated to reveal the greatness of past Roystonians and North Georgia Piedmonters. This unique page of history will never happen again, and must be recorded, not in traditional but in philosophical fashion. "Philosophy" means "Love of Wisdom" and that should not offend anyone, especially some Roystonians whom I have found to be philosophers.

My compulsion to write may be surpassed by my predilection to digress but even as a cluttered desk may indicate a cluttered mind, what does an empty desk indicate? After all, the mind does not operate in a straight line without crossroads and segments enlarging and enhancing the journey. I encourage others to take pen in hand and leave something for the future. I guarantee that old folks won't write trivial matters. Consider the following:

[Young Man to Old Man]

"You are wasting your strength with building here,

2

PRE-GAME WARM-UP

The year was 1978. I was in the middle of a political race in Alabama when my national fraternity called me to a business meeting in Pittsburgh, Pennsylvania. I was Southern Division President over thirty-one university chapters from College Park, Maryland to Lafayette, Louisiana. At the time, I did not feel that it was a good time to go, but in retrospect I am pleased because the event in some measure has led to my writing these reflections.

I arrived by plane in the afternoon, took a cab to the Hilton in Pittsburgh and got some needed rest. The next day would be comprised of morning business meetings and an afternoon as the guest of John Galbraith, owner of the Pittsburgh Pirates at a game with the visiting St. Louis Cardinals. So the next morning I dressed for the business of the day and went down to the coffee shop. The coffee shop was full of guests so I waited for an opening. At that moment a hand went up from a foursome booth beckoning me to join two young men. I responded and sat down with Roger Freed and Lou Brock, both Cardinal players.

We chatted about baseball, our origins and Alabama. Lou mentioned that he had played minor league ball in Alabama and wanted to know whether Alabama was my home state. I told him that I attended elementary and high school in Royston,

never had to follow Yogi Berra's admonition "When you come to a fork in the road, take it:" Many of these angels are in the background of my memory, several are in the foreground;

To those in every generation who remember and teach that "History is Prologue" and sadly it repeats itself because no one was listening in the previous generations. They are prophets, not geniuses, who simply recognize the signs and the trends;

To one of my heroes, Pambo the Idiot. Pambo went to Rabbi Hillel (contemporary of Jesus of Nazareth) and asked "Teacher, what must I do to become educated?" Rabbi Hillel responded "First, you must learn to control your tongue. Return tomorrow for Lesson Two." Many days, weeks, months and years passed but Pambo did not return. One day Rabbi Hillel was walking down the street of the city and encountered Pambo. "Pambo, why have you not returned for Lesson Two?" "Teacher," Pambo replied sadly, "I have not yet mastered Lesson One." Pambo was not an idiot!

To Horace Greeley who wrote

Fame is a vapor,
Popularity an accident, and
Riches take wings:
Only one thing endures
And that is Character.

ACKNOWLEDGEMENTS

To my parents and ancestors who gave me life.

To Grady and Louise, my brother and sister who never made it beyond childhood. I never knew them but I miss them and hope to see them on the other side;

To my enemies and detractors who, intending evil, propelled me to self-improvement and worthy goals;

To my family and friends who aided my journey to improvement and worthy goals;

To my soldier heroes and heroines who fought and died for my freedom even though they did not know me;

To my children and grandchildren who have praised my successes and have forgiven my shortcomings.

To those angels who stood at every fork in the road and pointed to the correct path: "the road not taken" never bothered me and now does not bother me. I

Prologue

'The past is prologue' - Thucydides

I have struggled to remember and to describe the years between 1934-1946. I hope to write about my experiences after WWII but that will have to wait. I have collected these memories over the years and put them together although in many cases, the segments just don't fit together. Life is not a straight line but more like a mosaic or a grid which has to be viewed piece by piece. Sometimes I identify myself with Johnny Cash's song that tells about his building a Cadillac by bringing home parts one at a time over the years from the General Motors plant and they reflected model changes. What a curious hybrid emerged from his collection of parts!

The success of this little book may depend on the memories I hope to receive from my readers. I shall print another edition to include my readers' collection from parents and grandparents. Let's not lose the foundation of modern life. People in their seventies, eighties and nineties have much to contribute.

Best wishes as you read "Sharecropper's Son." Look for my mailing address inserted in this volume.

The Author

Introducing the Sharecroppers Son

Bert was born October 1, 1931, the eleventh of twelve children of William Albertus (Bert) and Martha Olbon Hayes. His parents were sharecroppers. After years of study and travel he earned a Ph.D. in Middle East Studies (Hebrew and Cognate) with studies in Ohio and Israel. Below are some comments on author, book and man. (The reader may note that no *New York Times* best selling authors are quoted.)

"Dr. Hayes grew up in the North Georgia Piedmont with few amenities and opportunities: I grew up in the same conditions in Harima, Kingdom of Jordan, near the Syrian border. Both of us earned high degrees in order to serve God and Country. I recommend the author and the book." Major General Abdallah Soudi Bawaneh, Royal Jordanian Air Force, Retired, Gulf Shores, Alabama.

"I, too, grew up working my way through every episode of life and it was good for me." Jerry L. Unruh, Vice Admiral, USN Retired, Pensacola, Florida.

"Don't let that Will Rogers self-effacing 'Aw Shucks' demeanor fool you, this author has a message or two, or three...Dr. Hayes was not a Marine but he could've been." John L. Pipa, Lt. Colonel, US Marine , Retired, Magnolia Springs, Alabama.

"Dr. Hayes is the Mark Twain and the Henry David Thoreau of our times. His book is a *tour de force* and an international *panache* of achievement. No one else could have brought to life the Georgia Piedmont, the economy of sharecropping and images of WW II in the manner and style so comfortable to his personality." Mildred W. Caudle, Ph.D., Professor Emeritus, Athens State University, Athens, Alabama.

"Dr. Hayes, you have written a masterpiece but it pales somewhat when I think of your genius in looking through a stack of applications and coming up with a prospective employee who excels in duty, durability and loyalty. Your genius is also apparent in inspiring students to great achievement in academics and character and the 'little big things' you do for children that help them grow into responsible, productive adults." Linda D. Daniel, MS, Staff, University of Alabama, Tuscaloosa.

Your journey will end with the ending day,
You will never again pass this way;
You've crossed the chasm deep and wide,
Why build you this bridge at eventide'?"
* * *

[Old Man]
"Good friend, in the path I have come,
These followeth after me today,
A youth whose feet must pass this way;
That chasm which has been naught to me,
To that fair-haired youth may a pitfall be;
He, too, must cross in the twilight dim-
Good friend, I am building this bridge for him."

I believe that Royston has something to offer the next generation. I hope those who follow me will find their roots in the past and grow their own tree. It is disgraceful to think that Hollywood, Broadway, Paris and Television might determine their values and outlook. Having been born in the Thirties and having become a teenager in the Forties, I feel more relaxed about those days of poverty and uncertainty than I do about America's future. Sure, we didn't have much in those days but we had something. We joked about the Sears-Roebuck catalog's being a "Wish Book" or a supplementary toiletry in the Privy. Today we quip that a "Recession" is a condition in which we temporarily do without what our parents never had! I know how I longed first for a tricycle and a few years later for a bicycle that I saw in the "Wish Book." Those bicycles were marvelously illustrated with

3

cotton, his proprietorship changing to tenantship and sharecropping.

In retrospect, I now regard Royston as rural but in my early years, I elevated Royston to a city even though there were no large supply or department stores. Rural people still used the term "trade" in lieu of "buy" and "sell."

Not only did I learn the early Royston language from my parents but also I was able to form images built from the language. Moreover, I was familiar with the mule power, hand tools, dirt roads (either dusty or muddy), wood and covered bridges, campgrounds, brush arbors for religious meetings, evangelists of the stature of Lorenzo Dow, Billy Sunday and Dwight L. Moody. I never had a traditional childhood but learned to exploit my older brothers (#'s 1, 2, 3) to make toys of the early Royston era such as wooden wheel wagons, tom-walkers (stilts), string balls, poplar whistles, fishing poles and a whole repertory of games and farm duties. Consequently, my life did not differ significantly from early Roystonians. Occasionally we would take the mules to be shod at a real smithy shop. Those lean, tough Freeman boys could trim and tack shoes like the 1800s smiths. In addition to being oriented to the seriousness of life and the reality of death, I saw the contiguous unfolding of the culture as virtually unchanged from Papa's youth. I was wide-eyed at the threat of impending war and totalitarianism and much of the non-Royston world was brought home from time to time by my philosophical and athletic brother who worked on the pipelines of Texas and Louisiana and as a forester in the northeast Georgia mountains. Papa and Mama were very proud of him; I was more amazed by his contact with unknown places and species.

The drama of Papa's world played out in soil depletion, financial market crises and the depravity of loose living. In 1950, I stood in front of the building in Asheville NC, where Thomas Wolfe grew up. I thought about his book "You Can't Go Home Again" and reflecting on my home in North Georgia, nostalgia evoked some eternal words from my memory "For of all the sad words of tongue or pen, the saddest are these 'It might have been'." I reflected upon the harshness of the thin soil, the road banks exposing red clay, the thin tuft of topsoil where only the wild plums gave their meager offerings to a small lad trudging down the road in July, knowing that beyond the embankment lay more thin topsoil and depths of red clay, where once the gum, maple, hickory, oak, sassafras and dogwood grew. Early Royston had been depleted along with the soil. People kept striving to eke out a livelihood: many were stingy, bitter and occasionally ill tempered. The introduction of row crops, guano and boll weevils to an area unsuitable for such was unfortunate.

Now a growing population must migrate to Atlanta or Greenville and if they wish to come back to Royston, they must artificially create in middle

Royston what was natural in early Royston. The home that sent you away prepared you for better things.

Even when I was a youngster, the unpainted shiplap house boards turned from gray to deterioration, the tin roofs rusted and sagged, and many were converted to hay barns or simply abandoned. "This Old House" became a sad reminder of an unrecoverable past. I remember all the whimsical, reflective words. One day Papa and I were plowing cotton with a grass-removing heel sweep with one mule pulling. He came toward me and I toward him on another row. We stopped to rest the mules and chatted. His words are immortal: "Son, when we stop plowing the grass from the cotton and plow the cotton from the grass, North Georgia will make progress."

"Dear Papa, the cotton has gone: Chicken houses furnishing ammoniated manure enrich the fescue grass and the red hills are now green. The streams along the watershed are not so crimson. There's a little more profit (not much) in the business but the ecology is better. Are you listening, dear Papa?"

There are yet vestiges of the row crops for old terrace lines contour under the grass like serpents or pipes and sometimes in fields and yards, the grass is thin and the red clay shows its passion to survive. In many cases, brick has replaced the siding on homes and more often subsistence living is disguised by lawn and lawn furnishings that poorly hide low income.

To me early Royston is my pride. I don't despise the new, yet having to see through this artificial and inferior facade inhibits my vision of the past when the giants lived - namely, Mama, Papa and Ty Cobb. My brother, the third son from the Rock, also stands among the giants and will appear in a subsequent chapter.

I saw tears in Papa's eyes when he was reflecting on Royston's solid past. Nostalgia is common nearly everywhere, but there was more than nostalgia with Papa as he saw the passing of a generation which was strong in mind and body, which was proud of country, kith and kin.

MAMA, PAPA AND TY COBB

From Thomas Gray's Elegy (1750).
"Let not ambition mock their useful toil,
Their homely joys, and destiny obscure;
Nor grandeur bear with a disdainful smile,
The short and simple annals of the poor."*
"Full many a gem of purest ray serene, the dark
unfathomed caves of ocean bear;
Full many a flower is born to blush unseen,
And waste its sweetness on the desert air."

Mama and Papa were heroes; Ty Cobb was a hero and a celebrity. Respectively, they were born in 1895 (Mama), 1887 (Ty) and 1880 (Papa). All studied under the same instructor, Hershel Cobb, Ty's father. Hershel Cobb is my hero also. I attended grades 3 - 11 on College Street, the new school that Hershel Cobb inspired by his skills and presence. Royston built tough, moral people who realized that "my best helping hand is on the end of my arm." In this age when people are looking for handouts, Mama, Papa and Ty weren't even looking for a hand up. I really become weary of those people who sit like a baby bird in the nest, *boca abierta*, waiting to be fed. And some, recognizing that their ancestors had been deprived, want compensation. Mama and Papa never asked for relief even during the Great Depression (or the Grand Depression) even though they had ten children to care for. I really am angry with the 1920s generation, which fiddled the economy away and brought such miseries upon the '30s. I fear that we are now creating calamity for the generation of the early 21st century.

In retrospect, the generation of the '30s developed a philosophy of survival and the principal technologies continued, enabling America and Britain to be the driving force in silencing Hitler with the arsenal of democracy. Those who reached twenty years of age in the Depression came out of the coal mines, the cotton fields, the ranches and every walk of life to kick Hitler and Tojo in their dictatorial philosophy.

Mama, Papa and Ty Cobb were at their finest after the turn of the Century. Mama came from hard-working stock. Mama's father of Dutch ancestry, the "Dutchman" as he was called, had principles and dignity. In the course of fate, he married a lady of Scot and Cherokee ancestry. The Scots came to Appalachia as bachelors and married Cherokees. Travel Northeast Alabama, Tennessee, Georgia and Carolina and you will see many Cherokee faces with Scottish names. The obvious is, and this was known in pre-Christian Centuries, that females tend to resemble their fathers and males their mothers. This is not 100% but the percentage is large. Mama followed the Dutch side of the family, her brothers the Cherokee. I can see my maternal uncles now with their black hair, dark eyes, tall stature and heavy forearms. I recall their piercing eyes looking at me and through me when I was a youngster as if to say "Well, let's see what we have here and what's this kid going to amount to?"

Mama, Papa and Ty Cobb grew up in an age of responsibility and duty. Today we have rights and preferences. Today's world revolves around "likes" and "don't likes." Listen to the parents "Honey, do you want to? Do you like?" Often young people's opinions are "like" and "don't like." The sum total of youth conversations involves rights and preferences. Youth expect to be compensated for fulfilling obligations. They also expect bonuses. The words of Jesus I paraphrase "after you've done all you're obligated to do, you're up to zero." The disease is epidemic.

Years ago I heard the concept overseas. I was on a public bus in Israel. Seated behind me were two youngsters going to school. Their conversations were replete with Ohev "like" and Soneh "dislike." I was learning modern Hebrew (I had already studied Classical Hebrew) so I tried to get all the words. Both youngsters hated "kevaker". I took the word back to my linguist friend, Werner Weinberg. Werner had taught me German so I could pass my comprehensives in graduate school; furthermore he was fluent in Hebrew. He chewed "Kevaker" slowly and his eyes lit up - "Well, doctor," he exclaimed, "This 'kevaker' is to be expected: they don't like oatmeal!" I have to tell youngsters occasionally:
"There are three words I don't like."
"What are they?"
"I just told you."

Then there's the "blame" generation. "It's not my fault." Everyone is innocent and pure. It's always someone else's responsibility and someone else's fault. The generation of the '20s will have to pay for the misery they dumped off onto the '30s. Their "grasshopper" philosophy brought havoc to the hardworking families. Black and white farmers suffered because of the devalued dollar, speculation, disdain for collateral and the droughts and dust storms. I shall have more to say about the '30s ("The Grapes of Wrath") and the mid-life of Mama and Papa. Somebody must pay for the times they went hungry so that the malnourished kids could eat, for the times their teeth ached and their bodies were weary without compensation.

I hear the younger generation complain about their predicament because their predecessors were discriminated against. I personally don't feel deprived: I feel very sad (and indignant) that my sharecropper parents and older siblings were deprived. Sure, we didn't even know we were poor until we went to school in town where the merchant's youngsters attended. The Country people bought (as said before "traded") in town and could always buy one item for the price of two! So when the discount businesses started after the War (the real war), who were the first to complain about unfair business? Right!

I felt that I knew Tyrus Raymond Cobb. My parents knew him and often talked about his strength, determination and intelligence. Imagine a Southerner making the big leagues only forty years after the Civil War and only twenty years after "Reconstruction" (in reality "Exploitation") of the South. The early Ku Klux Klan (probably Greek Kukleo or "circle") was against exploitation and oppression by Northern opportunists. Would that Abraham Lincoln had lived.

So Ty Cobb arose out of what could be called the "outback" of the South, not the South of Plantations and Slavery but of vigorous yeomanship, which had run its course by the '20s and sadly depleted in the '30s. I have only an impression of the great Ty Cobb: I have daily visions of remarkable and awesome clarity about Mama and Papa. I see them working, standing in silence looking with those famous penetrating gazes at us children, wondering, "What hath God wrought?" I, when reflecting with "that inward eye" wonder about them "What hath God wrought?"

What is this life of Mama and Papa? We ask, "Who were they?" as they must have asked, "Who are these creatures about our feet?" In eulogy to Mama, my kid sister wrote beautiful words about the Mama/sibling relationship: each sibling holds a mystery and a bond according to my sister. I was a special mystery to Mama with my "auslander" views, dreams and career.

I remember when I was in college, many of my conservative friends scoffed at the English poet, Wordsworth. In his youth he was an activist and greatly embraced the French Revolution. In his maturity he was disillusioned with the temporal and tried to get a grip on the eternal. What manner of "creeping Buddhism" did he embrace? For me his words were haunting in his "Intimations of Immortality".

"Our birth is but a sleep and a forgetting; the soul that rises with us, our life's star,
Hath had elsewhere its setting,
And cometh from afar.
Not in entire forgetfulness,
And not in utter nakedness,
But trailing clouds of glory do we come
From God, who is our home…"

Dear God, should I sleep and forget again to emerge upon this earth, please burst me forth into the home of two sharecroppers and my siblings. The question of "Life before birth" and "Life after death" are more ponderable than the staggering blow "Is there life after birth?" I swear by the empiricists, I remember very few of my experiences. So when philosophers say we're only a collection of memories, I've had very short life! Now you may quit reading here or you can show your courage because eventually I shall take you through the conscious, the sub-conscious, the unconscious, the stream of consciousness (James Joyce) in addition to the actual events that shaped my destiny. I owe this to my parents, my siblings, my children, my grandchildren and a few of my colleagues.

I really feel sorry for those whose parents were just necessary utensils and utilities to bring them to adulthood through the rites of passage. My Mama and Papa were vehicles of eternity. They were not educated beyond their intelligence but combined the inherited morality of their predecessors with the practical (and often urgent) matter of surviving. This contrasts with the generation since World War II who feel that full-time employment in one's field is guaranteed by the Constitution and Bill of Rights. I will have more to say about the origin and nature of the Bill of Rights.

So… what can we say about the matrix and milieu of Mama, Papa and Ty Cobb? We can reiterate that they were yeomen who grew up in a good latitude with a good attitude. The soil was at its finest with the opening of new ground. They grew up off center from the Civil War and had their own fix on the times. One of my dear aunts used to quip that her predecessors were cowards, yet the truth was that the Civil War did not greatly affect the lives of the yeomen who did not participate in the antebellum cotton economy but were drawn into the post-war production.

Moreover, all were a part of the movement of migration from Virginia and the Carolinas further south and west. The Scots married the Cherokees but how the Dutch came into the picture I don't know. My kid sister contends that Grandpa (the Dutchman) was actually a Swede and appears on a manifest of 1818. I think, on the contrary, that 1818 marks the birth of

Great Grandpa William Harmon in the paternal line in northeast Georgia. Now, who Great, Great Grandpa was I have no clue.

The context of settlements in northeast Georgia was near springs, but wells became more prolific at the turn of the century with vertical production, population growth and settlement on the "rises" or elevations surrounded by the new fields. Breezes were better on the higher ground especially through the red and white oaks but wells had to be deeper. I can still hear the spin of the windlass and the bucket hitting the water, moreover, milk could be an inner container tied inside the bucket and could remain during the day or night to raise the cream to the top for churning into butter.

Moreover in the Piedmont context of Mama, Papa and Ty Cobb, character was developed by the patient use of human labor, which gave a sense of confidence and sound sleep to the participants. Lack of stress, physical labor and more than just a modicum of success in the soil enhanced longevity and *bon vivant* (or may I add *joie de vivre* since there was a certain French influence in those times).

If my memory has not deceived me, I think the cemeteries in and around Royston bear out the longevity of the people born in the late 1800s. Someday I shall take pen and paper and walk reverently through those sacred places and record names and dates. I know some of those names will be my relatives and some the families of my classmates at ol' Royston School.

MAMA

Mama was the Dutchess with Cherokee brothers - Cherokee brothers who did not take kindly to Papa's taking their sixteen year old sister to wife. Papa was thirty-one, the oldest of eight, and with the unexpected death of Grandpa, had been virtual father to the family. God knew that we were going to need this mature, industrious and intelligent mother who would be trusted with twelve children, dutifully raising ten to adulthood and sorrowing over two lost to unknown disease about 1920.

On the first day of spring, 1914, Mama at eighteen bore her first-born, a son. There followed a second son in April 1916 and a third son in November 1917. Papa said, "If the war continues, my sons and I will go to defeat the Kaiser." As it happened, two of the sons, the second and third, left home to fight Hitler and Tojo. I shall devote much time to the third (Third Son from the Rock) as my pen reaches forward.

Mama was proud of her first three (and subsequent nine more), and made them clothes to wear and bought them each a yellow Ty Cobb baseball cap. The first three were the children of the parents prime and throughout life we younger ones could feel this mystique and we were proud of them, not envious.

Oh yes, the yellow baseball caps... Papa also had a buggy (carriage) with driver and passenger seat, a "rumble" seat in the rear for the three little ones and a fine gelding horse "Dan." On Sunday, they went to Poplar Springs campground for religious services, as was the custom. It was an eventful Sunday in the summer of 1919, for someone from Royston was there with an automobile! Even though Ford and Rambler had built since 1903 (?) nevertheless, not a great number had reached the Georgia Piedmont. The service ended and the crowd watched as the "Model T" clattered onto the Royston Road. Mama put her three boys with their yellow Ty Cobb baseball caps in the rumble seat, climbed into the passenger seat while Papa untied Dan from a sapling and soon they departed. Dan was in good spirits and head high he set up a canter to Royston. A cloud of dust appeared in the road ahead: the dust was created by - yes! You guessed it - the Model T.

Well, Dan didn't like dust anymore than Papa did; in addition, the little yellow baseball caps were taking on the powder also. Papa's attempt to pass the "T" was initially unsuccessful but suddenly the road widened and Papa whistled (his whistle was extraordinaire!). Dan flattened his ears, the harness raised on his arching back and like a tempest gaining momentum, he pulled alongside the "T", then beyond the "T" and before Papa began to soothe and reign Dan in, they were just a speck in the distance relative to the "T."

I think it was the next day (according to the Third Son from the Rock) Papa met the fine "T" gentleman in Royston and quipped "Didn't I see you on the road from Poplar Springs yesterday?" The fine gentleman was equal, yea superior to the quip "Indeed! I wondered who that was with the three cantaloupes in the rumble seat!"

Mama never laughed, but you should have seen her discreet smile and sparkle in her gray-blue eyes. In these early days before so many children, low cotton prices, drudgery, fatigue... the smile undoubtedly emerged more often, yet it was always possible. The Third Son from the Rock was like his mama, did not laugh but smiled, and had the Hayes Gaze, invented and patented by Mama. Mama never scolded, reprimanded or gave advice; she simply had to look at us, and we figured out with our own sensitivity and intelligence our commissions and omissions, and we were dutifully repentant.

Mama was the original ecologist. She used, re-used and recycled. When the youngsters had an opportunity to earn a small amount of money she would invariably say with an Appalachian gerundial, "Be asavin'."

"Save your money" has rung in my ears for sixty-five years and it's still the best truism for poor folks like me. How I regret not heeding this whimsical suggestion from this great lady, the survivor of poverty, pestilence, flood and drought. She was never the recipient of retirements, investments, donations, relief funds: she had stared hunger and starvation directly in the face and knew the value of saving, put the "a" back on the gerundial, "Be asavin'." In memory of my mother, I say "ZIKRONAH LIVRAKAH." You might find this expression on a Jewish tombstone.

Seemingly acquiescent to the uninformed, she sometimes showed me a different side... resolute silence. "Go figure" as the kids say. Papa was exactly the opposite and I'll say more about him later. Mama was a believer in fixed mores, aphorisms, axioms, proverbs and commandments. It was the Dutch-Cherokee way. Like the Third Son, you should have heard her listen. It was like a silent thunderclap. Whole conversations (and except for the Third Son, we were all motor-mouths) would suddenly cease because Mama was listening so loudly. We could suddenly become accountable as if taped or filmed to be exposed to the public.

I often think of Mama's silence like that of Sir Thomas Moore, the thorn in King Henry's side. "And what does Sir Thomas say of my intentions?" asked the King of his Counsel. "Nothing M'lord, nothing!" "Curses" whined the King, "his silence thunders up and down the land."

The Second Son had a special place for Mama. He left home at fifteen and went to work in Atlanta. He would come home to the little watershed farms, often with an auto, sometimes a motorcycle. Most of his time on these visits would be devoted to Mama. He and Mama would plant and work in the garden, even planting the flowers Mama loved, making sure the rambling rose bush climbed the fence. Mama liked to add some beauty and femininity to the harsh environment of the erosion, row crops, parched earth and dim prospects of a good year. For this the Second Son is commended. He was the sophisticate coming home to share with his Piedmont Mama.

I'm more Jewish than Gentile when it comes to Time and Space. Gentiles see their parents and ancestors moving out ahead to that mysterious realm beyond the River: "There's a land beyond the River, that they call the Sweet Forever..." but Jews see the children being pushed into the future while the parents and forefathers drop off behind. Now, my children don't think your old man weird - these concepts come from the philosophy of time and space. The aborigines such as the Australians push (figuratively) their ancestors back into the "dreamtime" and their presence is felt at those times when the ancestors' lives are called upon for wisdom and learning. They inhabit the fields and streams, the earth: we are living on their sacred ground, their creativity and their cumulative experience. St. Paul (a Jew) writes in the Christian Bible, the Book of Hebrews "For inasmuch as we are surrounded by such a crowd of witnesses [our departed folks] let us run the race that is set before us..." Mama does not "come back to haunt." Mama's image is there to the extent that I listened to her silence, her acts of sacrifice and devotion to those she had committed to rear up.

Listen my children... I do think I angered your grandmother, my mother, on one occasion but I know

33

she forgave me. It was during WWII. Papa was well beyond his prime and a life of tough physical labor limited him on the hillsides of our watershed farm (perhaps "farm" is a misnomer). I was a skinny, undernourished youngster who tried to keep the crops going and the family fed. I was so thin that "if I sat sideways in school I was counted absent." My mule knew I was weak, and just about every day she wheeled about on the cotton row and went to the barn, dragging me and the plow through the plants. I'd had enough and as Popeye says, "Enough is too much."

On one particular day, the mule and I were harrowing cotton and the tines of the harrow were freshening the ground and occasionally scratching up the crabgrass. After thirty minutes, the mule made an executive decision to return to the barn. "Bad idea" as my grandson says. I began to turn the harrow over and over in the same direction, winding the traces that came back to the singletree until the traces tightened around the hindquarters of the mule, which continued downhill. Soon she could navigate no longer and fell into an erosion gully where I punished her with a convenient stick.

Mama, hearing the commotion, had come out of the house onto the porch and was quite startled by the scene. She cried out passionately for me to spare the brute's life. Yet the mule had sensed my lack of authority and my weakness and had taken conscious advantage of my state. I, too, realized that the strong brothers had gone to war and that my aging father could no longer be in the fields so I wished to do my part. How could I contribute if this creature, the hybrid beast, which had neither pride of ancestry nor hope of progeny, upset my designs on patriotism and winning the war?

Moreover, I realized then, and more especially now, that my meager efforts to effect the economy were only great thoughts and not production. So much can be written about the mule, the hope of the South after the Civil War and the prolificacy of cotton even as William Faulkner realized "... the mule, that plodding, patient, loyal beast that will serve you faithfully for ten years for the opportunity to kick you once." Or, Mr. Faulkner, to leave the field when she is ready and without my consent is unpardonable!

So Mama crossed the yard and the spring branch and made her way up the hill to view the struggling mule in the gully, wrapped in her harness and braying piteously. Avoiding the front hooves, I reached under and unfastened the hame strap on her harness and collar, which summarily peeled off and left the mule comparatively free. She struggled to her feet, trembling and subdued. I noticed the muscles in her neck were corded and they remained so until her death. Mama took her by the bridle and led her to the barn, removed her bridle and let her go to tremble, graze or drink, whichever she chose.

Mama never mentioned the incident thereafter: she needed not for I remembered every detail. Mama had known the mule from the time Papa and the Third

Son from the Rock had gone to the auction in Hartwell to buy them at depression prices or maybe to accept them from President Roosevelt's Rehabilitation program. There were many mules there and most of them were larger them the two mare mules which parked head to head in a corner and kicked the heads off hostile mules crowding them. They weighed about 900 lbs. each in a corral of heavyweights.

The mule that made her own decisions about quitting time was a story in her own right. The other mare mule willingly proffered her feet to be shod by the Freeman brothers in Royston, but not my mule. Papa never let us ride the draught mules anyway, for his theory that pulling the load caused the animals to be dependent upon the load to keep them from falling, and when they were used as mounts they occasionally stumbled and would injure us.

Of course, Papa's theory was not the reason we (or no one) rode the mule of my discussion. She could buck like a machine at Gilley's in Texas. I remember climbing and sitting on a rail at the corral while a boastful cowboy (allegedly from Montana) affirmed, "If you can get a saddle on her, I can ride her." Well, my brothers found the saddle and bridle and held the beast steady and our aforementioned cowboy climbed on with an air of confidence. After a brief pause, the air of confidence metamorphosed into the upper air. A sunfish of springload arched, straightened and our cowboy shot into the ozone and landed without control. Dazzled but furious, our cowboy, an unbeliever of the first order, pleaded for another chance. The scene was even more electrifying. I was certain that none could survive the latitude and longitude of his propulsion. There was no third attempt but I heard words never uttered by my Protestant parents or siblings.

Please pardon this excursion so now I shall return to Mama. Now you may say that a woman who bore a dozen youngsters (one set of twins) surely was not bright and certainly in the process of time was not attractive. Wrong! Many young men resented Papa's theft of her in 1911 and though I never became conscious of her until twenty-five years later, I detected a romantic and creative spirit about her evinced by a wry sense of humor. Never a gossip nor mean-spirited person, she could humorously describe a neighbor with a faint smile that fixed the graphic in my mind forever. About a domineering woman who lived east of us on a high hill she mused, "we don't get any sunlight until Ms. X allows the sun to rise." The Second Son inherited her marvelous spirit but not her reluctance to vocalize. He could describe one of our contemporaries as a "well dressed farmer who still has his plow shoes on" indicative of the breakdown in style among us. The culture dressed "a la mode" but with one modicum missing. I do miss the Second Son, too.

Now, let me tell you that a fine, educated, polished gentleman in our county (or a neighboring county) was accused of having a "crush" on my mother of twelve children since 1911 (?). This was never proven nor were there any overt scenarios, yet... When my mother passed away, this legendary gentleman attended her funeral with noticeable reverence and sorrow. Go figure!

Any of Mama's children would travel great distances by any means of transportation, and moreover crawl the last hundred miles to see her. I am so eternally grateful to my older siblings and even two of my brothers-in-law who cared for my mother while I was career-building and earning a Ph.D. in Middle Eastern Studies. Mama was told that a Ph.D. degree was being conferred upon me. "I'm not a bit surprised" she casually (but I know Mama) replied. The inner smile of contentment and pride was there (I know my Mama).Life is not a straight line: there are intersections and grids so Mama will appear again and again. This monument to womanhood and motherhood cannot be duplicated but she can be emulated. Do you hear me my children? In my mind and experience (that's French Rationalism and British Empiricism) I see Mama's whole life from a female child born in the vigorous, nutritive late 1800s to a woman worn by child-bearing, the Great Depression, the death of her sons and daughters, self-sacrificing quotidian duties and bombardments against physical health and strength, and who undoubtedly remained an emissary of God.

PAPA

I don't miss the dinosaurs! (I'm really one myself, being an anachronism in thought and practice). There's a lot of concern these days, some real and some camouflage, about the extinction of certain species. There was the snail darter at Tellico, Tennessee, the owl in the Pacific Northwest, the beach mouse on the Gulf Coast, etc. I'm concerned, too, about extinction of species and languages that have been lost. I studied the Sumerian language, which survives only in clay pictographs, or logographs found in Southern Iraq. No other language is even close to the vocabulary, structure and syntax. Yet the Sumerian culture survived. Their need to measure to re-identify the sites and properties of Southern Iraq following a flood was obvious. They devised the circle and sexagesimal system. Measurements from the center in increments of six are now found on our compass (6 x 60) and our analog watches or time pieces with twenty-four hour days and at the equinox, twelve hours of day and twelve of night.

The above is a whole study in itself and I'm glad I spent some time and thought with this mysterious culture. Yet, the Sumerians are now extinct: the culture survives in geometry, picto/logo writings which were borrowed by the Semitic peoples and were first reduced to syllabaries, thence to the Alphabet, the first wonder of the world.

Then there's Papa. Since he was fifty-one when I was born, I grew up with a dinosaur, an anachronism. We called him "Papa" while my less fortunate contemporaries had "dads". I have mentioned Papa briefly and eventually along the way and even now I feel I cannot give him the treatment he deserves. His fifth son and eleventh child (yours truly) just does not have the literary ability to put concepts into print, however, here's a feeble gesture.

I never remember Papa when his hair was not gray. I saw old photographs of this six-footer, straight as an arrow, proud but not arrogant, his blue eyes penetrating beneath dark brows. He was pictured with my grandma, two brothers and five sisters whose names are still elusive for me. What a striking picture he presented! I used to worry about my slow growth and eventual size, and he would say, "Pshaw, son, I was born premature and three and one half pounds. It was January (and Royston gets cold) and they, thinking that I had no chance to live anyway, bundled me in a basket and put me behind the wood stove near the wall to die warm. The midwife proffered me a chunk of fat meat, I began to suck on it and have been eating since. I was about thirteen before my pores opened up. I suffered from red face and was always near explosion. Finally my pores opened. I was relieved but no one could get close to me, the stench was so bad."

Papa was right. Now at two hundred pounds, slightly slumped shoulders and brought an inch or so lower by gravitational pull and heavy lifting on farm, factory and sports, I'm still appreciative of Papa's words and those of Abraham Lincoln "A man should be tall enough to reach the ground with both feet."

Papa was the loquacious flip side to Mama's restraint and was always demonstrative of Professor Hershel Cobb's pedagogy. He was very gregarious, and in his youth played a banjo and sang duet with his younger sister at gatherings of all sorts. (He sold his banjo when my growing brothers were spending more time "plucking" than plowing.) Papa continued to sing at the campground, the brush harbors and the church. I can still hear his strong voice at the New Franklin Christian Church (Disciples of Christ) near Grady School (the two-room, six-grade school where several of us attended). Papa was friends with all, rich or poor, black or white, male or female. He had his limits, too. An acquaintance (but apparently not friendly) intended to drag Papa out of Papa's buggy. Papa reached under the seat, drew out a pistol, put it on half cock and said, "That's far enough." The man was glad not to die that day and departed.

Papa never owned an auto and as the family grew and he was "under the lion's paw" of sharecropping, the buggy and the horse went also, so it was the wagon (buckboard variety) that went to town for supplies and to haul cotton to the gin. Thank you, Papa, for letting me go to the gin and wait in the long line of mules, wagons and sharecroppers who gathered in smaller units to talk about the weather, prices and whether Beechnut was superior to Brown Mule. When we were able to move in the queue to suction up our own load of twelve or thirteen hundred pounds of raw cotton, the operator would allow us to put our heads close to the vacuum pipe to pull our hair up and he would joke "that'll rid you of lice and nits!" Papa would chuckle because Mama was always perspicacious and had her own agenda and methods for ridding us of those abominable lice.

No buggy, no horse but Papa could walk. I could hear his stride a hollow away, those long legs in rhythm with the occasional kick at a stone in the roadway. Papa knew our walk, too and slowed on those rare occasions when he took me with him to see a neighbor about a trade or a service. During WWII when the older boys got a pass or a leave, they would come across the front porch in the middle of the night and Papa would say "that's X" and true to his knowledge of the stride, he would be right.

In spite of his tough upbringing and rather vigorous early years, Papa could be compassionate and gentle with children, beasts and certain political issues. Yet he was adamant in his position regarding socialism and the concomitant Nazis in Germany. The "Brown Shirts" and the "Red Shirts" were not his choice of apparel. When the First Son came home (as I've mentioned before) my big ears would be filled with philosophy and politics. I began to be aware at six years of age of the impending doom of society, a sort of worldwide apocalyptic Titanic sinking into the realm of the unknown.

Our neighbor had a radio. How he obtained it or could afford it, I don't have a clue, but there was a battery and perhaps it was a Motorola or such. I suppose Papa and my neighbor had always been friends but as far as Papa was concerned, the friendship should not end. I had the special privilege of accompanying Papa down that dusty road to listen to the Joe Louis vs. Schmelling fight. Of course, all were pro-Joe and anti Nazi. Later I was to learn that Schmelling was not such a bad guy, and even the alleged kidnapper of Charles and Ann Morrow Lindberg's baby son may not have been the kidnapper.

How this country Papa read the pulse of the whole world, I'll never know. Much of it was the occasional return of First and Second Sons to the cotton field home and then Papa's contact with anyone in the outside world (Royston, Lavonia, Hartwell, Greenville, S.C.) who produced some heretofore-undiscovered News.

In spite of our poverty and isolation, victims of the Depression would come through the country, carrying their hoes (later called hoe-boys or hobos) to help in the fields, get a meal and a nap in the hay barn, then move on to other opportunities. For the most part I observed them from a distance yet occasionally one, missing his own nephews, kids or grandkids would rumple my towhead and make conversation with me. Of course, Papa would talk at length with them, garnering information from the outside world; Mama would scrape field and coop and make "Nail Soup" (or was it "Stone Soup?"). Mama, unlike Mother Hubbard, knew how to scrouge (old Southern word "squeeze + crowd").

Once Papa had nearly a dozen kids to provide for, he was under the "lion's paw" (who wrote that story?), and probably had to take a lot of gaff, which offended his dignity and bearing. But having a sense of dignity and principle, often he encountered a point beyond which he would not go. He never failed to let the older ones know what choices they had and arrived at a consensus so that he could deal with the situation. I told you Papa had a good vocabulary but occasionally when his principles were threatened, he uttered epithets and ultimatums "Rather than do that (such and such) I'd rather eat s--t and run rabbits." So there! Only occasionally he would utter the "S" word such as when one of the kids was associating with questionable companions Papa would bellow, "If you play with a t--d, you'll get s--t on you." So there!

Papa was also a Sunday man and usually found in church. During the war, he for the most part did not require me to go to church and luckily one Sunday I did not go. One of our cows was ready to "freshen" and when the parturition began, she was having problems delivering so I ran quickly to a neighbor's in the village and a kind gentleman came (his grandson is now a Major League Baseball catcher) and helped me "pull the calf." This was my first midhusbandry and I'll forever be grateful to the neighbor for his help. Papa and Mama came home from church, and I remember Papa's smile and congratulations for saving the milch cow and calf. When I get to the world to come I hope that neighbor is still my neighbor.

Papa and First Son were very close. Even when a little fellow, First Son following Papa through the field to find a neighbor a good melon, cried our Papa's first name, "Hey Bert, here's a big one!" Yes, Papa was always influenced by the Big Guy's input. They would argue at times, too, in the most civil manner. My six years old ears tuned in.

First Son:	"But who made God?"
Papa:	"God has always been."
First Son:	"Everything had a beginning."
Papa:	"Not God."

I'm sure that the conversations were deeper yet my memory is that of a child. Then there was talk of war...

First Son:	"War with Germany is coming."
Papa:	"We have to win this one."
First Son:	"I'm thinking about Argentina. Some of my oilfield pals are there now."
Papa:	"Argentina will be at war too."
First Son:	"The next war will be fought in the air. You can bet on it."

At the mention of Argentina, some of the older siblings joined in. I had never heard of Argentina. I knew it must be farther than South Carolina where First Son planned to work and play baseball. When he was home, he was always putting make-up games together with the locals he had grown up with. He had lettered in several sports at Hartwell High. His Latin was good, too. I never understood his nickname "Sack." I suppose he tackled the quarterback often. First Son never went to Argentina nor to the war: While returning from a baseball game with several other players, he was killed in an automobile accident on Buncombe Highway near Greenville, S.C. in June 1940. Papa and Mama never fully recovered.

I knew Papa only in his decline but I suppose I was a sensitive youngster and needed only part of the picture to construct the remainder. Later, as I talked to my older siblings and even my younger sister who lived at home four years after I left, I believe I had gained a true impression of his years before my childhood. Papa occasionally took a strap or peach tree branch to me when I deserved to be punished but he never punished unnecessarily. He always emphasized, "This hurts me worse than it does you." At the time I didn't think so but now that I have children I know 'tis true. I'm pleased that he heard me out one day until I could explain my innocence. We had a millpond, which powered an overshot wheel about a quarter-mile down stream. Severe weather threatened and Papa told me to go open the sluices to keep the water level down during the flood. I went up the millrace and pulled two of the main sluices. The storm passed and there was no rain. Seeing that there was no rain, several boys from the local two-year college put the sluice gates back, raised the water level and went swimming.

That night there came a real "gully-washer," a "frog strangler," a "Noahic deluge", and the next morning, Papa and I were on the verandah and saw the creek unmistakably carrying the logs from the millpond. "Son, I told you to pull those sluices!" "But I did pull them Papa." Papa was not convinced but gave me the benefit of the doubt and later found out the truth. Well, we switched to motor power for the mill and the wheel was silent forever. The overshot troughs rotted away and today only the dug race can be found like the ancient canals of Iraq.

My children, you may read the preceding pages and make your own profile of your grandfather. There's some of him in all of you and you can be proud of his stately bearing, his uncompromising morality, and his philosophical and practical leanings. Remarks and insights about your grandfather will certainly emerge. Note that I don't use proper names to great extent. A genealogy and list of proper names may appear in the Addendum and you, if challenged, may "sort them out." If not challenged, you may not have read this far!

TY COBB

The name is synonymous with baseball but it is more personal with me. "Ty Cobb was one of the first names outside my family that I remember. Since his records began to fall one by one - season stolen bases, lifetime stolen bases, lifetime hits, etc., his name began to be known outside Royston and outside the baseball world. A few years ago typing in "Ty Cobb" offered some eighty thousand "hits" on the Internet. This was the name I grew up with and my contemporaries and I aspired to be like him in skills and temperament.

Few people can distort an image, as can politicians, news media and Hollywood. When I began seriously to study Cobb's life in connection with my writing, I was amazed that so much clutter, exaggeration and abuse should collect like barnacles to his name. So I said to R. M., a colleague and Detroit Tiger fan, "What's your impression of 'Ty Cobb' the movie?" "Don't go see it if you admire Cobb the way I do" moaned R. M. "The movie has distorted the life and times of a great performer."

Well, I know what sells in the popular world: sex, violence, drama, intrigue and unfortunately, misrepresentation. One may call it Mendacity. Had Papa and Ty Cobb returned from the dead, they would not have recognized the characters. By analogy, Jesus and St. Paul would not recognize Christianity nor

Muhammad, Islam.

Look it up: Casey Stengel knew that Ty Cobb was the greatest. "I never saw anyone like Ty Cobb. No one even came close to him as the greatest all-time player: that guy was super-human, amazing." While you're studying the Piedmont Plateau and the unique features of Royston's environs, drop by the Ty Cobb museum on Cook St. near the Cobb Memorial Hospital and see and hear the testament to his character and record. Like many Roystonians, Ty rose to the pinnacle of his career through great determination and lesser skills.

Then there's the scum that would impugn Ty's character. A friend happened across some pollution from the Internet called "Ty Cobb: The Song." I'm not going to reprint it here. It is disgusting, nauseating, repulsive (those are moderate descriptions). The writer lacks style, vocabulary, thought and decency. There's even a copyright but don't worry - - no one other than the filthy, will copy this filth. It's your call: "Ty Cobb" by Chris Cornell, performed by Soundgarden c 1996, A & M Records, Inc. Luckily also on the "net" is the real Ty Cobb, Master of thought and language.

"In legend, I am a sadistic, swashbuckling despot, a Draco of the diamond, who has waged war in the guise of sport. The men I went against didn't call me a dirty player, that charge has come from those anointed with the critical power developed through carrying a press card. The truth is that I believe, and always have believed, that no man in any walk of life can attain success who holds in his heart malice, spite or littleness toward his opponents. The competitor who comes armed with right in his heart and mind has nothing whatever to fear. The honorable way is the only way."

"Ole Professor Cobb" did his "job" on Mama, Papa and Ty. Listen to the classics as Ty explains his idea of retaliation:

"But I did retaliate. That I freely admit. If any player took unfair advantage of me, my one thought was to strike back as quickly and effectively as I could and put the fear of God into him. Let the other fellow fire the first shot and he needed to be on the qui vive from then on. For I went looking for him and when I found him, he usually regretted his act - and rarely repeated it. I commend this procedure to all young players who are of the aggressive type. The results are most satisfactory.***

"Along with the counsel of my father, I fell back on Polonius, when in Hamlet He advises Laertes, "Beware of entrance to a quarrel; but being in, bear't, that the opposed may beware of thee." "No better guide for a ball player ever was written."

Most writers like to show how aggressive and uncompromising Ty Cobb was. Moreover, he was regarded as a racist. Just remember that without toughness and persistence, no Southern lad could have played major league baseball in the North only forty years after the Civil War. Who was really prejudicial in those days?

The classics quoting, peanut (goobers) - eating, fun-loving outfielder metamorphosed in the Big Leagues the first year in Detroit. Not only was he a rookie, but also he was a Southern rookie in Detroit. Pranks, ostracism and incitements began to push him further and further into isolation off the field. He had no political or diplomatic tendencies that could ameliorate the situation. Were it not for his dedication to baseball and to becoming the best in baseball, he could easily have taken another three-day ride on the train to Georgia. His teammates and opposing players determined the role that he would play throughout his career, viz. neither asking for nor giving any quarter. It was almost his silent manner (sometimes taken for conceit) which announced "If that's the way it's to be, so be it. Baseball is my life and I'm going to live it."

Now all the details of this seemingly contradictory character can be found in biographies and newspaper articles (I shall admit that many of the sports stories favor the person and actions of Ty). I am for the most part trying to demonstrate how Royston and the Piedmont shaped his innate and some of his acquired personality prior to his big league career. I also praise him for his unselfish contribution to Royston in his ebb tide while suffering from cancer and other disappointments. I like to think that there was enough of the Old Royston left forty-five years after Cobb's birth to start me on a road to achievement.

Mama, Papa and I have certainly bent more to

exigencies and compromise than Ty but we still share the matrix and milieu of his origins, character and temperament. As demonstrated in many lives, Hershel Cobb the father must be the great hero but the lesser celebrity.

Another incentive, of course, for Ty to succeed at baseball was his father's hope that Ty would tire of baseball and return home to be a doctor, or lawyer, or soldier. The very week that Ty broke into major league baseball, his father was killed. Having promised his father success, he pursued baseball with fervor. Religiously Ty felt that his deceased father was still watching. Ty was more than just another Southern lad who made the big leagues. He simply grew out of the bone and sinew of the Piedmont Plateau in a post Civil War geographic and economic development.

REVIEW OF ROYSTON AND THE PIEDMONT MATRIX

You've now been introduced to the emergence of Royston following the Civil War - the pioneer energy of the late 1800s and the transition from springs and subsistence to wells, cotton production and the decline of soil, the economy and to the yeomen. Now I shall present my case again with hopes that my children can screen out the post WWI additions and see the raw ingredients of this my origins.

First, the streams and springs were essential. The streams could be counted on in the rainy months yet the springs rarely dried up in the drought and although some were reduced to a small effluent. Even Royston was known as the Franklin Springs until W. A. Royston gave his name to an intersection near a proposed Railway line.

With the need for horizontal production of cotton, springs, still important, could not meet the needs of the horizontal spread of indigenous and immigrant population (Ty Cobb's family had moved in from Banks County, a county which shares a small portion beyond Interstate 85 at "Banks Crossing.")

Now the plateaus were more desirable for cotton expansion because more contiguous acreage with longer rows could be gained. The watersheds were less desirable even though more creeks and springs were there. Water had to be found on the plateaus so well digging became the answer. In some parts of the U. S. in those days cisterns were more practical but they demanded a more elaborate roof, gutter and catchment cistern. I saw a number of these in the Midwest of the U. S. and in the Middle East. As a matter of fact, I've seen underground cisterns in the Middle East large enough to float and paddle a boat in. The area was not desert but had rainfall upwards of twenty inches.

So the Piedmont went to wells. Few of the well boxes and windlasses remain today. Many have submersible electric pumps and supply homes beyond the City Water system. In my childhood as we moved from one sharecropper shack to another, I remember the well, the creek and sometimes the spring.

Diesel and gasoline motors had advanced with the automobile so cotton gins, large and productive, made use of the motor for ginning. However, water power for grinding corn and syrup remained until WWII and as a novelty still appear in Tennessee, but I don't know of one in the Georgia Piedmont. Creeks could be dammed or groined and sluices or millraces could route water to undershot or overshot wheels whose axles or shafts turned cogs which governed the turning of a stone wheel over a static stone. Fascinating! Dams were a better idea for low-volume streams.

Syrup mills were generally powered by mules pulling a bar or beam in a circle, a beam attached to cogs which turned twin vertical cylinders which squeezed out the juice from the cane much like the old wringers squeezed water out of cloth. The squeezed stalks of cane were called pummels. The juice was then transferred to wood fired evaporators, the juice pushed along a labyrinth of runnels until it emerged cooked into syrup at the other end. O the joy of a lad whose family had a millpond, a millrace and an overshot wheel to turn the stone to grind the grain.

The corn mills I remembered were Cromer's Mill on a NE to SW watershed creek in Franklin County, our own on Franklin Springs Creek in Franklin County and Mason's Mill in Madison. The Mason Mill exterior structure still stood in the year 2000 yet the other appurtenances had been removed or had deteriorated.

By the 1920s, most of the plateau land had outgrown "New Ground" status yet the watersheds were still producing some. From the outset "new ground" or the 'sheds could provide only "patch" cultivation such as a "patch of corn" a "patch of beans," or a "patch of cotton." Second Son at home for a visit was trapped into a government survey of acreage and crops and was quite amused that allotments never appeared in "acres" but in "patches." This phenomenon spelled the ultimate demise of the watershed for other than subsistence. Watershed bottomland, not suitable for cotton anyway augmented non-cotton production. Farmers had to fight vigorous wild growth in the "bottoms" but grain and corn grew very well.

Apart from the "new ground" expansion, one has to be mindful that topographically the Piedmont was more bound by its overall soil type. The foundation, ultisol, was its destiny. Ultisols are well developed geologically and also lie under more transient "new ground." Red or yellow ultisol (communities "Red Hill" or "Sandy Cross" respectively) dominated the region. The red soil has an interesting personality and at the surface may have the consistency of axle grease and glue and the properties of dye. Pulled up wet by the plow, the red soil may harden into clods and can be broken up naturally by rain water saturating, freezing and then crumbling with the thaw, otherwise the farmer must "clod hop" during cultivation and will do so all spring, summer and fall until a sufficient wet freeze comes around. As you will see, what happened after WWII obviated the "ritual of the red", for the economy changed dramatically. The trees that were cut, the land that was cleared, the earth that was exposed to the horizontal expansion of cotton, "the cash crop", was to be no more except in a few domicile areas where landscaping was neglected. The old poem we recited in the 1930s.

"The old red hill of Georgia,
So bald and bleak and bare,
They have no robes of venture…."

If anyone remembers or locates the complete poem, please let me know. By paraphrasing we might add a refrain:

"The once red hills of Georgia,
So bald and bleak and bare,
Are now robed with fescue grass,
And prolific vegetation fair"

One transformation was brought about by cotton and the other by soldiers returning from the war who diversified the economy by working new farming practices, and occasionally supplementing with "working in town."

So the landscape has gone full cycle in the Piedmont with the exception of replacing trees with grass. On the other hand, beginning with the Piedmont and reaching into the Blue Ridge, there were some things which did not change: natural shrub and trees maintained their beauty of varieties or green in the spring and awesome colors in the fall. Few people from the Piedmont travel to New England to see the fall spectacle. I have been in New England in the fall but not to see the foliage, although I must agree that the hamlets in New Hampshire and Vermont nest in tranquil beauty in the fall; nevertheless, there is absolutely nothing that compares to a Piedmont-Blue Ridge Fall.

Northeast Georgia boasted a plethora of bush, vine and tree. Spring displayed five or more shades of green - pine, cedar, poplar, oak, sycamore, gum, hickory, maple, sassafras, beech, birch and ad finitum. Fall bombarded and awed the senses with the entire possible spectrum. The variety competes with and surpasses all known foliage arrangements in the world. Some of my favorites were the gum, maple, sassafras, sumac (shoemake) and yellow hickory.

Not just the colors captivate the senses: the stateliness of the tulip poplars, especially near the streams were latitude high and longitude wide. The dogwood, pink and wide, could not hide among the shelter of pines and hardwood and in the lap of nature rivaled the planned landscapes of Northeast Atlanta. Along the streams were the ubiquitous creek birch, muscadine, and fox-grape ("frost grape" in New York State).

"Fox-fire" also grew on the stumps in the damp woods and on a moonlit night they glowed in the dark. The "fox-fire" was "phosphorous" and I never made the connection until I lived in Cuba where matches were referred to as "fosforos" or phosphorous. Along the creeks were also the weeping willows, which my little daughter referred to as "hanging down trees."

As youngsters we knew the rarer varieties of bush and shrub: chinquapin, buckeye, grandfather beard, sweet bulbs, sugar berries, poke berried (the adult poke salat), mountain laurel (which goats occasionally browsed on and got ridiculously drunken). The Royston variety of sumac matured in the fall with a salty seedpod, which resembled the head of syrup cane. The leaves were burnished orange and red and most spectacular. The pokeberry also produced berries, which were used by Native Americans (and also by us youngsters) to paint objects and faces.

Most of the beauty of North Georgia is not edible but it certainly boosts the psyche and pride when living conditions are otherwise miserable. I often thought of nature as the enrichment of the soul when undernourishment and uncertain occupational realities were discomforting. I look back upon my early days with good feelings about the Piedmont and the Blue Ridge. As I've said before, I've been around the world.

Review the Royston area with me:

1800s - Heavily wooded with sparse population.

1900s - Acreage opened to cultivation and especially cotton.

1940s - Reduction of cotton acreage and the beginning of ground cover grass and diversification.

1950s - Increased diversification in the rural scene with rural people also working in light industry and service.

In the course of covering the ground and stopping erosion plus aspiring to have a practical application came a blessing and a curse - KUDZU! Brought from Asia before 1900, it was introduced into the Piedmont in the 1930s to help contain erosion, but not being properly understood, the best advantage was not taken of this marvelous vine. Kudzu was (and is) a very valuable vine, not only for erosion control but also for nitrogen replacement and animal feed. The Asians use Kudzu sprouts as a vegetable. I tried to identify the sprouts served to me in China several years ago, but I'm not sure I got the right translation. Our local folks in the South felt threatened by the plant, which climbed trees, fences, buildings, roads and "slow-moving Southerners." K. S., a neighbor of mine in Georgia, solved the kudzu problem on his farm by turning out several thousand white Holland Turkeys to graze; in two years and two Thanksgivings, one could not find any evidence that the vines had ever been there. K. S. now operates a super farm at Watkinsville, GA, but I don't know if he's utilizing kudzu or not. (I understand that Kudzu also has medicinal values but I have not researched that aspect). Kudzu and grits have become Southern features subject to both praise and ridicule. One might say, "Kiss my Kudzu" as well as "Kiss my grits." In my opinion Kudzu still has a real future. I remember an anecdote about a farmer in Oklahoma who asked his son-in-law to get that black, oozy stuff off his farm because it was messing up his livestock's water holes - the son-in-law obliged and became an oil baron. Maybe a Kudzu baron will come forth also.

The above reflections certainly glorify aspects of the Piedmont plateau and landscape. On the negative side the creeks and rivers never boasted quality game fish. When the rivers ran red, we sought after sleepy channel cats in Cromer's Mill Creek and the forks of the No. Broad River. In several of the creeks, the horny-head suckers nosed up small stones and gravel from the creek bottom for spawning beds, hatched out red minnows which the locals called "Red Horses", which resembled gold fish until they matured. A number of the mature fish were required to "stink up a frying pan" and their bone structures prevented good filleting. I don't know whether the horny-head is extinct or not. I hope it's still there but droughts, toxic runoffs and infrequent rains may have caused their disappearance. They may have died out for lack of a case, for lack of a defense.

The game animals were basically the rabbit and the squirrel, not impressive game but sometimes a necessary fare to supplement the diet. In recent years the attempt to introduce the White-Tail Deer to North Georgia's rivers, creeks and branches (creek tributaries) has been highly successful. In my youth we never saw the White Tail anywhere but from the 1960s onward, they were everywhere with increasing population and boldness. Like kudzu, I hope the Georgians find a way to turn curses into blessings.

Moreover, I do not wish to overly romanticize life around Royston especially from the farm boy view: April and October were the decent months and often with the knowledge of what was to follow it was difficult to enjoy them but we learned to make the most of them. April throbbed with life and promise. The earth was cool and the air was warm. In elementary and middle school we had already shed our shoes even though occasionally we had to shift from one foot to the other to keep our feet warm until the school bus arrived. We had awakened that morning to the sounds of spring, smelled the freshly turned earth by the plow and perceived the new greens of the shade trees outside the window. Who we were we had no clue but to be alive and part of the universe was a delight in April. In my teaching career I had a colleague at the University of North Carolina who always traveled to "Old England" in April. I chided him and sent him pictures of "Old Alabama" in April. Of course my colleague was devoted to Robert Browning.

Oh, to be in England now that April's there, And
whoever wakes in England, sees some Morning,
unaware,
That the lowest boughs and the brushwood
Sheaf -Round the elm tree bole are in tiny leaf
While the Chafffinch sings on the
Orchard bough
In England - now!
(from Home Thoughts, from Abroad [1845].

After April, we faced heat, insects and humidity. Experience is a damaging memory, which saddens anticipation. Did you ever milk a cow in the heat of summer? The cow has declared war on biting insects with tail, feet, and pendular head while you sit there on a stool practicing damage control (and collateral damage). One has to be able to move quickly when the foot comes up, then down to keep the errant foot out of the milk pail. The swish of the urine tail is indescribable. Either hold the tail with one hand and slow the process or endure the swish while milking with two hands.

Some Quakers (Society of Friends) befriended me while I was in college in Pennsylvania so I feel it's permitted to write this anecdote. A Quaker was having the same problem with a cow like the one mentioned above, and finally gave up trying to milk the cow. He picked up stool and pail, walked around to face the cow head on: "O cow, thou knowest I am a Quaker hence I will not curse thee; thou knowest I am a Quaker hence I will not strike thee. What thou dost not know O' cow, is that I'm going to sell thee to a Baptist who will beat the h--- out of thee. (All due apologies to Friends and Baptists.)

Then there's October... I support Helen Jackson's impression:
"O suns and skies and clouds of June,and flowers of June together,Ye cannot rival for one hour'October's bright blue weather."
(October's Bright Blue Weather, Stanza I)

And who in North Georgia can deny William Carman's feeling:
"There is something in October sets the gypsy blood astir."
(A Vagabond Song, Stanza 3)

We were still picking cotton in October. We waded through the early morning dew, which dissipates with the equinoctial sun. The sun tans one side of the face on a contour row and the other side on the return. The smell of the cotton burr and leaf are in the air and if we're lucky, there's a late maturing melon in the adjoining field. The sky is azure and the air is champagne. The sumac is becoming golden and orange with streaks of red. Some who never picked cotton complain (and lie) about the ordeal but for us the family was in the field, having fun with what the boll weevil left for it would mean new denim clothes and shoes for the winter. Occasionally, we raised our heads about the row to pull lint from a stubborn boll and whizzing through the air would come a "Maypop" or the fruit of the passion plant thrown by the bazooka arm of one of the brothers.

Perhaps October is just another month in Royston now. Is that good? The old October can never be restored because the economy, focus on nature, the pace of life and the value systems of old are gone. Old October is not celebrated in Oktoberfest as the German community in South Alabama does. The old October was not imported: it grew directly out of the ground and out of the past. It was a time of harvest, a time of reflection and a time of preparation for the exigencies and harshness of the winter, especially for us who lived in poorly heated homes. In winter, we didn't burrow in like Russia or the Yukon waiting for spring. We lived with the winter, too. In my post-high school youth when I hitched in the winter to Wisconsin to work in the automotive industry, I marveled at how the people there were mechanically and materially prepared for the winter but they were probably less physically fit than the Georgians I knew.

So, how about it Royston? You don't have to (neither can you) live in the past but without a knowledge of it, you're trying to build the second floor on a vacant lot. Have a little respect. Make regular visits to the cemeteries and see who they were and the epitaphs written for them. Get off your "Island" and find the mainland of your inheritance. You newcomers to the Royston area, acquaint yourselves with the spirit (and Spirits) of the past and to repeat Thomas Gray:

"Let not ambition mock their useful toil, their
homely joys, and destiny obscure;
Nor grandeur hear with a disdainful smile,
The short and simple annals of the poor."

The greatness is in Royston as it is in every place on earth. It is now obscured by a new generation and an imported or migratory population that may locate its values elsewhere.

Well, here I go wandering again and I don't want to lose you (if you've gotten this far!), so I'll go on to other matters of which you have only an historical knowledge but no personal or analytical connection.

FAR BACK IN TIME

Now there are some who can trace their ancestors back to Ezra and Nehemiah or at least to the Mayflower but as one savant told me "You don't want to trace your ancestry back very far: they either swung by the neck or by the tail." So I will go back only to 1818 when Great-Grandpa was born. I think his peregrinations were in South Carolina as well as in North Georgia. He lived until about 1880 I understand, and is buried in a now unmarked grave in Eastonolle Cemetery near Toccoa, Georgia.

Great Grandpa was married to four wives, not at the same time of course, and I think Grandpa was the son of the second wife. Grandpa was born in 1852 and hence was a little fellow during the Civil War. Great Grandpa and Grandpa had an encounter with a Yankee patrol, perhaps in South Carolina, and the story I heard was as follows: They were driving a team of oxen pulling a wagon along a country road and a Union patrol crossed the road. The soldiers knew the family-type was not hostile but they detained the boy and teased him while Great Grandpa ignored them and moved on down the road. About a hundred yards distant, Great Grandpa stopped the team, called to my Grandpa-to-be and said "Come on William Howard. Those Yankees will let you go or I'll come back and take my bullwhip to them!"

The Yankees laughed, and shuttled the boy on the

way. I think this is a fair representation. My folks in South Carolina and Georgia, like the Free State of Winston (Winston County, Alabama), were off the beaten path of the War and were not part of the plantation and slave-holding societies. My family always regarded themselves as Americans. The story is told of the great abolitionist Henry Ward Beecher (1813-1887) that while lecturing in Britain after the Civil War, was interrupted by a heckler who shouted "Mr. Beecher, why did it take the U. S. four long years to defeat the rebels?" Ward let the twitter settle down and calmly but with emotion replied, "You must remember, Sir, that we were fighting Americans!" We descendants today can truly say that we had very tenuous connections to the political war.

I do believe Great Grandpa would've laid lashes upon the Yankees with his bullwhip, losing the battle of course, but winning the respect of the Yankees. The War was a tragedy: Civil Wars are even more tragic than wars with foreigners. Americans should not be fighting with each other and should certainly be united when engaging the foreign enemies. To my disgust I have heard treasonous talk when, for example, the Democrats are fighting the Republicans during wartime when we should be united.

Well, either Great Grandpa's third or fourth wife belongs to a sinister plot, in fact, if her designs had succeeded, I would not be writing these memories and you would be spared. An independent genealogist of another family verifies this story so I can tell it with certainty. It seems that wife Three or Four had a grudge against my grandfather and her other stepchildren and decided to murder them. She was able to find arsenic and cooked it into a batch of biscuits. Great Grandpa smelled a peculiar odor and threw the biscuits into the yard. According to Papa, the ducks in the yard "covered them up" and soon were falling over dead in the yard. What happened to the wicked stepmother, I am not sure, but I hope she got her just desserts. Mrs. W. called me and asked my about the incident and I verified the story as told by Papa.

So, you see, I know very little about my grandparents but I know them to be of good character and conviction. Grandpa was a worker, splitting logs for railroad crossties and raising a great family, Papa being the eldest.

The most famous story about Grandpa's principles was his abhorrence of human excrement left indiscriminately around Poplar Springs campground. The ladies had the luxury of chamber pots, but the men took to the woods. Grandpa was very careful not to step in the human waste, but once it was unavoidable. Upon ascertaining what had transpired, he simply took out his knife, reached down and cut his shoelaces, walking out of the excrement without ceremony. "Cutting the shoelaces" has been passed down from Papa to all of us as symbolic of what to do with a bad and uncorrectable situation. "Cut your shoelaces and get out" is a clarion call. Papa taught it to me and I have passed it on to my children and grandchildren and I hope the tradition and practice continues. An admonition is added: "Cut your shoelaces and try your very best to prevent its happening again."

My Grandpa also was known to take a nip occasionally because those were tough days and one needed to "take the edge off the pain" at the end of the day, yet like Papa, he was temperate, in control and besides, his horse didn't drink so DUI or DWI were never an issue. One of Grandpa's sisters married into a family that imbibed more then their share of the Georgia "Moon" and strangely enough, all lived one hundred years or more except poor Uncle Joe who lived only 93 years. I had not heard about Uncle Joe for a while so I asked my brother, the "Third Son from the Rock" what happened to Uncle Joe. "Drank himself to death" was his laconic reply.

I understand that not one of my siblings knew their grandparents, even the siblings born before and during WWI. This is all too tragic for me, so today I make a big thing about being a grandparent and a big "to do" about grandparents in general. I just don't know what will happen to our society when the current grandparents pass on to their rewards. Today babies are having babies, and the babies have to raise themselves. It's certainly precarious.

I think my grandparents left me a legacy exemplified in my own parents and the good blood of Cherokee, Scot, Dutch and English ancestors. They were poor people of outstanding principles, a love and kinship with the English language and exercised decent articulation from an adequate vocabulary and were not ashamed of refinement. They were true examples of "poverty does not necessitate bad language and behavior." I have found that with a good education one can explain his poverty with greater eloquence. Fortunately in America poor people can attend good public schools and if there are not too many student nuisances distracting them, they can learn. Unfortunately, young people only know about their "rights" and not their "responsibilities." Like the generation of the 1920s, they grasshopper, not bee and ant, through life and blame the government for misfortune. In the "Roaring Twenties", the fabric unraveled and people blamed it on the Hoover Administration. President Herbert Hoover was a fine engineer and businessman. He had the foolish notion that hard work and less government could revive the country. The country opted for more government and asked, "What can my country do for me?"

So, in the simple scheme of life, my grandparents had a tremendous advantage. They did not spend a lot of time in formal education yet they were able to read, write and cipher. Their contemporaries in the world of science and technology were harnessing electricity, sound waves, combustion energy and locomotion - the principles of such enduring to my day. The quantum leaps have been in nuclear fission, cybernetics, genetics and astrophysics. In the world of labor, unions have improved conditions but in turn have become abusive and counter-productive. The pendulum swings back and forth in America: it is the same pendulum and can be identified by close observation.

INTERLUDE

THE THIRD SON FROM THE ROCK

"He ain't heavy mister: he's my brother." I can't say everyone has such a brother or someone in his or her life whose existence, "thereness," and whose ongoing presence so permeates life's experience. I became cognizant of the Third Son when I was two and a half years old. Third Son shuttled us down into the pasture at Pea Ridge sharecropper farm in April when my youngest sister was born. A year and a half later I remember him climbing to the roof at the Adams Place to receive buckets of water from Papa and the older siblings to put out a fire that had started near the newly fired chimney, which was burning off the accumulated soot from the previous winter.

In those years, I did not remember Sons One and Two because they were seeking their own fortunes in Texas and Atlanta. Third Son never sought his own fortunes anywhere: he simply fulfilled his destiny of being in loco parentis to a host of undernourished siblings who trailed after him. As a son, I trailed more often and more closely to this quiet, hard working blessing from God. He was my angel. Before the

Renaissance put halos and wings on angels, they were simply "malachim" to the Hebrews. They were envoys or messengers sent by God. They just appeared at the appointed time like the malachim who came out of the desert and announced to Abraham and Sarah that they would have a son in their old age. Sarah, listening behind the tent flap, was so amused that when the son was born she named him Isaac, "laughter."

Hence, an "angel" is not the Renaissance concept but simply human types dispatched by God to aid His people in need and distress. Where they come from and where they go sometimes is a mystery. I have heard hundreds of stories from rational people who describe receiving assistance from strangers who were not even there to receive thanks after the event. The Third Son, though, was always there and even when serving his country in WWII, sent money home to help his siblings.   On the subject of war, the Third Son was inducted into the army at Fort McPherson, in Atlanta, on February 14, 1942 and honorably discharged on February 14, 1946. I missed his presence terribly so I wrote to him every week at Camp Little Rock, Carson (Colorado), Pendleton (California), Polk (Louisiana), Meade (Maryland), and then to Greenland where he engineered with the Danes. In the military, he, like a great number of lads who matured in the Depression, was absolutely obedient and cooperative with a spirit of patriotism and an urge to kick the enemy so he could get back to the little family farm and brighten his corner of the world.

We are indeed a collection of memories. Some are very elusive, dim, and come to us like an olfactory memory, yet in the case of the Third Son, the memory is continuous and vivid. Not only was he the one on the roof putting out a fire but even in his acquiescence, agreed to accept enough money from Papa to fly in a Piper Cub when a barnstormer landed in a local pasture and offered rides. I was about five years of age but I remember the smile (he never laughed) on his face when he came home. He would've been a great pilot but money was just not available and when he went into the military he had been plowing furrows and harvesting crops until the last minute when he was called up by the draft (conscription). Papa told me a story about the Third Son. He hardly talked at all until he was four or more but he knew the words. Papa and sons had been to a neighbor's looking at a new litter of pigs and upon returning home Third Son was very "worked up" about something and only mumbled. "What do you want son?" No answer. Again. No answer. Finally Papa remembered the pigs…."You want one of those pigs down at Mr. B's?" Nods. Nods. Nods. So, Papa took him in hand and went down to the neighbors and bought him a pig.

I learned much from the Third Son. I was his shadow and probably his burden. After sixteen years at home, I went into the world as First and Second

Sons had done to seek opportunities. I would return home as often as possible to work with my "angel." Most likely, during my visits I would not see neighbors or boyhood acquaintances, spending all of the time working with him. He built a new home after the war, cut the timber, logged the sawmill and hauled the rough lumber to the planing mill. He wired the house for electricity that eventually came from Georgia Power. I helped him all I could. He was the best.

I remember just about everything he ever said. The weather was cold, rain turning to sleet and I with my thin hands and he with his thick and calloused would be repairing barbed wire fences. "Goodness, Doc," I complained "Why are we fixing fences in this weather?" "Too wet to plow" he said, brief and curt like a New Englander except for the amused smile on the lips that never laughed.

On another occasion I would suggest we were overdoing some job and opine, "Let's leave out this option, Doc." He would look at me with compassion in his eyes and say, "We're going to do this even if it's RIGHT!" Fellow builders loved his slow, plodding, careful work in brick, block, framing, electrical. Contractors might try to rush him but would hear, "I've got only one other speed and it's slower." He didn't have to look back: his work was good. We were also roommates. During the thirties, we were the only sons at home so he inherited me. Most of the sharecropper homes boasted a kitchen/dining room combo and two bedrooms, a double fireplace - one fireplace faced the kitchen and the other the first bedroom. The houses also had a front porch, or verandah as Papa called it, which stretched the length of the front of the house. We would enclose the porch on one side, roof it with tin and create another bedroom. Third Son and I would room together there. He would also take boards or timber, bolt them together, provide or improvise slats, sew mattress covers together and stuff with corn shucks, wheat or oat straw. In the winter, we could sink down in the mattress with one of Mama's quilts and we fared reasonably well. In the summer when the porch room was stifling, we often moved a palette to the porch and listened to the night sounds. Occasionally in the fall, we had front seats on meteor showers or "Shooting Stars." When summer turned into fall the nights would get colder and colder with winds from the Blue Ridge. A "no dog" night turned into a "three dog night" so eventually and reluctantly we shook the blowing snow off our quilt and moved inside to await spring. Third Son also built a chicken house. He cut logs, notched them and put up a structure about ten feet by twenty feet. I forget how he raftered the roof but he knew how to roof also. There was a local hatchery in Lavonia where he was able to buy the little fuzzy Chirpers and in about ten weeks, we had more protein to eat. I can still see the little house near the woods and a sage field. His inexperience showed somewhat when he did not peel the pine logs and they began to deteriorate earlier than expected.

Third Son shaped my future. He would not let me drop out of school as he had done to work on the farm. He sensed his divine angelship and made me stay in school. While in the army, he encouraged me "If this war lasts, join the Air Force - that's where the difference is." Well the War ended when I was fourteen or younger so I didn't join. At sixteen I took Air Force exams and did very well but when the recruiters came by Royston High and "looked me up" they also "looked me over" and because of my small stature "overlooked me."

Third Son always encouraged me to fly so when the opportunity came, I trained for General Aviation and got my single and multi-engine ratings. He was very proud of me but I was more proud of him. I love to fly and don't regret my relationship with flying but I'm more pleased to honor his ambitions for me.

You might be thinking that I loved Third Son to the exclusion of First and Second. NOT SO! First and Second were not excluded. We siblings were born over a twenty-year calendar so by time and space we formed nuclei of two and three. Third Son and I formed a nucleus with a fourteen-year age difference. I began to overtake him academically and eventually physically but I never caught up with his wisdom, character and contribution to the survival and successes of the family. He was probably greater than George Washington: President Washington could not tell a lie - Third Son could tell a lie but chose not to do so. He was not my idol on a pedestal - on the contrary he gained my respect for his demeanor and actions in very difficult circumstances and I knew him well.

Other siblings had different relations and different concepts. Almost all agreed, however, that he saved our family from defeat by our poverty. He was like the Rock from whom he descended. He had the same acceptance of life as it is and knew what to do to make it better. He inherited the "Hayes Gaze" which could do more to get my attention and correct the error of my ways without rebuke or punishment.

Those who did not know the Third Son well will regard my remarks as extravagant: those who knew him well will regard my remarks as woefully inadequate. He was in the military when I went through my tenth through fourteenth years. I tried to do the work he did while on the farm but it was too enormous for me. I also learned that the homeplace on the watershed could only be productive if we struck a mother lode vein of gold. When he returned from the military in 1946 strong, healthy and ruddy, I could see his future of loss of weight and vitality. He should not sacrifice himself to this futile topography. I encouraged him to "re-up" in the military so that he could apply his experiences to the defense of our country. I assured him that we could manage somehow to support our aging parents and ensure his future at the same time but he would not entertain such an idea. One of my sisters chided me for wishing him to go back into the military but in retrospect, I think I had a good point. We cannot change the past, so that's the way it happened. I watched my brother give his life to that farm but at the same time he gave his life to all of us.

I drove one hundred thousand miles in my brother's last years to help him all I could and to transport him back and forth to the Veterans Hospital in Atlanta. Friends and relatives were making bets about who would live longer - he or I. Some of my relatives thought that the attention I gave my brother was designed to acquire his property. This hurt me very much but since I have not been immune to hurt in my life, I was able to overcome because I would not let anything break the bond of brothers. The only legal connection I had with his property was at the advice of his lawyer, who looked us both in the face and advised my brother to sign over the property to someone trustworthy to keep it out of probate and family argument.

One of my critics is a niece, who otherwise is vivacious and quick-witted. In her perspicacity and infinite wisdom, she concluded that the Third Son had "a mean streak." Well, dear niece, what mortal does not have a mean streak!? The Third Son had helped raise three nieces, and since he helped raise me too, I can attest to how the "mean streak" grew on him. No one could raise that crazy niece and me without developing a "streak."

I left home at sixteen and returned only for visits.

My brother occasionally came and worked where I worked but Georgia kept pulling him back. He worked in Racine, Wisconsin when I worked in Kenosha, Wisconsin and when I moved to Pennsylvania and Ohio, he worked briefly while I was there. He failed to come when I was in Texas, Washington State and Cuba but our bond was strong. Deep in my heart, I wanted to get together with my older brothers and start a business. Sometimes large families are more fractioned than smaller families so partnership was never effected. It was difficult to put Georgia, Louisiana (Second Son) and Rambler Me together.

The early sons were never children. When Papa and Mama drove the wagons and smaller children across the county to another sharecropper farm, the nine, ten and twelve year old sons drove the cattle on foot over the country roads through curious neighborhoods and barking dogs.

On our last move through Franklin County when I was eight years of age, snow had begun to fall and after we arrived, the snow continued to about twelve inches. There was no food and no fuel. While some gathered windfall branches, Third Son went to the barn, wrapped burlap bags about his old work shoes, took his rifle and a bag and returned with twenty rabbits. We ate fried rabbit, boiled rabbit, rabbit fricassee and rabbit a' la rabbit for days but we survived. There was no neighborhood welcoming committee: We were on our own.

I can still see the way he walked. After years of walking behind the plow and approaching one activity after another, his knees were always slightly bent and his gait was determined. As a youth he played baseball with the older brothers and neighbors, yet work time was always greater than pastime so his gait was fixed. But his arm and hand - they were another matter because baseball remained in them. My son was about eight or nine and was playing Little League in Ohio. We were visiting the farm and I had set up an automobile tire in the pasture to let him practice throwing accuracy. He stood at about the pitcher's mound and threw. I retrieved and tossed the ball back to him. Third Son - and now uncle - was coming up behind my son in the pasture with his customary stride. I threw the ball back to my son and it went past him. Third Son picked up the ball, cocked his arm and threw the ball through the tire set on edge. He then proceeded to give my son a couple of hints on foot and arm position and release of the ball. He probably had not thrown a baseball in many years but his style characterized the youth of his day. They had less leisure time so they learned quickly and well what had to be done.

I'll never tire of talking and writing about Third Son, who ironically, talked and wrote very little but even his silence was deafening. Listen up grandchildren to hear about your uncle. A n i m a l s loved and trusted No. 3. The legendary Francis of Assisi had no more rapport with nature than No. 3.

Sure, he had to take his weapons and find us food in the winter, but he hated to kill. He saved the hides of animals, stretched them on tanning boards and didn't waste a thing. He built box after box for the bees until thirty hives dotted the edge of the clover and honeysuckle fields. He would frame the box and "Super", and occasionally lift the top and watch these amazing communists work. Bare headed and bare armed he would harvest the rich, dark honey. Whenever we heard a swarm, we would make a clamor to disorient the bees so they would come to rest on a limb. No. 3 would take the limb and all with the Queen Bee and locate them near a new hive entrance so they could set up housekeeping.

His reputation as a beekeeper was widespread. One evening I was visiting to take care of some of his needs when he was aging fast. There came a knock at the door and men from miles away came to visit. They had found a swarm of bees on a limb of a tree in their yard, wanted to capture them but were inexperienced "Would you come and help us?" I knew my brother didn't feel well but he said to me, "Go to the shed. There's a new box there. Please load it on the truck." He turned to the men and said, "Go on home and we'll follow you shortly."

We went to their place, No. 3 found a place for the bee box, spread a canvass in front of the box. Then he returned to the tree and carefully cut off the limb holding the swarm. He brought branch, swarm and queen bee back to the box and laid them carefully on the canvas. After "setting" the table, so to speak he added "They will probably move the queen in and occupy the box." "What do I owe you?" asked one of the men. "Not a thing. Good luck in starting a bee business."

No. 3 had the warmest, most engaging sense of humor. As in example, when we had the goatherd, one mother goat had rejected the kid so No. 3 brought the little one from the barn to the farmhouse to nurse it there. He bought canned goat milk to feed the kid from an infant bottle. I came home for a visit and discovered that he was buying goat milk. I determined to go milk the nanny and feed that to the kid. No. 3 wasn't too enthused about it but he agreed. Really, I am a smart and resourceful guy so I found a nanny, milked her, brought the warm milk back to the house and went through the procedure. The kid eagerly took a couple of draughts from the bottle, looked thoughtful for a second, then spewed the milk out. I looked incredulously at my brother to see his surprise. He was smiling his wry smile. He suspected all along what would happen. He often let me learn for myself.

Until the very end, he had the same gentle spirit. We had rushed him to the doctor for he had septicemia, congestive heart failure and showed the pallor of death. We then moved him to the Hartwell Hospital because the VA in Atlanta did not have a bed. The Hartwell Hospital, realizing the urgency of the situation, put him in a room and immediately one crew after the other administered aid. Blood pressure, heart rate, respiration, etc. were evaluated. The room was filled with technicians. Another young tech entered the room, not confident about when and where to start with his function. My brother noted his plight and said tenderly "Young man, take a seat and I shall get to you as soon as possible." All the apprehensions in the room disappeared and everyone laughed a laugh of relief.

I have picked my memories to tell about Third Son and my words are entirely inadequate. I must warn you that other memories will appear, which I shall record hereafter. Of course, I have many memories for which I have no words to describe. One of the reasons is that Third Son is more that just an "angel" person: he is also an institution of the pioneering days of Royston, the sharecropping era of The Great Depression and in addition, the role of hero from the past who lived in a more modern time. He was such an epic figure that the military did not have to teach him how to obey, to discipline himself nor how to shoot a rifle. Goodbye for now "Third Son from The Rock."

FOR SHARECROPPERS ONLY

Before I route you through the stages of my sharecropper experience and perspectives, you may wish to test your "Sharecropperness."

Answer each of the following with "YES" or "NO":

Your family was poor but rich in children

Your bathroom was an outhouse and an inside galvanized tub.

There was a washstand on the back porch.

There was "running water" … in a nearby stream.

The house was rarely finished and you could see the studs and rafters.

The floorboards had cracks and the house set on stilts.

The house and barn roofs were galvanized tin and the barn roof was used for sliding.Roofs also could be used for a game of "hand-over" in which a team on one side threw a ball over the house and if caught, the catcher could run around the building and throw the ball at the other team, hoping to leave an impression.

The yards had no grass but had generated a hard

packed sand in which circles could be drawn for playing the ubiquitous game of marbles. Now I shall create a paragraph of Sharecropper Characteristics.

The house was usually set on a higher level than the fields, boasted heat relieving oaks in the summer but these deciduous oaks offered little barrier to the winter winds. Other outbuildings might include a cotton house, a tool shed and a corn shed. You went barefoot nine months of the year and even to school until the eighth grade. You wore brogans without socks while plowing rocky ground. You never asked, "What's for supper?" but timidly and rarely, "Is there any supper?" You didn't really know you were poor because everyone in your two-room school was poor. You were given a quarter-dollar at Saturday noon and encouraged to "bring the change home." The girls wore dresses to school when society should've allowed them slacks and in the winter their legs showed the results of standing before an open fire. You know that cotton picking is only a third of the process from planting to ginning. You practice "NO-TILL FARMING" when you drilled in field peas (black-eyed) behind the wheat and oats harvest. You realize that I've left out hundreds of sharecropper characteristics and you're anxious to tell me some. If you answered, "Yes" to 10 or more of the above, you are invited to continue reading and reminisce with me. If you answered "Yes" to fewer than 10, read on - you must be interested or you wouldn't have gotten this far.

I was a sharecropper until 1940. I knew a few sharecroppers in those years. They were fellow students and neighbors. During and after finishing college and graduate school, I traveled extensively and met former sharecroppers, black and white, in my economic and cultural world. They are everywhere but like WWII veterans, they are going to another sharecropper planet in the universe rapidly. When I meet people I usually find out their background and it's amazing to discover how many were sharecroppers or the children of sharecroppers. This older generation, black and white, yields for me a lot of conversation and memories. I hope that I can print this inadequate account soon so that other sharecroppers can call or write me about their memories.

I was born in Hart County at Eagle Grove between Royston and Hartwell. I have seen a picture of the little house in the cotton field. Mama said that the mock brick siding covered up the log structure underneath. The log structure was certainly more attractive than the imitation brick. From there we moved almost annually to the following:
Pea Ridge --- c. 1933Adams Place --- c. 1935Sam Sloan Place --- c. 1936Estes Place --- c. 1937Parham Place --- c. 1939

So little was happening apart from sharecropping that my memory was not clouded with superfluity. I remember Pea Ridge where the youngest and caboose to the train was born. I remember the lane that ran down to the main road and to the left was a little church for the black people. Papa occasionally would take us there because he loved the church and the songs. Papa was gregarious and a great singer. More than just incidents and events, Pea Ridge fixed the Sharecropper land, the isolation, desolation and a peculiar beauty in my psyche.

The following year or at least after harvest we moved to the Adams Place. There were a number of memories and impressions there. The road ran very close to the house. There were oak trees in the sandy yard and Mama used dogwood limbs tied together to keep the yard swept. Also in the side yard, was a well with a cover, platform and windlass. The well was probably about forty feet deep and tapped the first water table. I can still hear the whirr of the windlass and the splash when the bucket reached the water. It was the same well that provided water to put out the chimney and ridge fire when Third Son was the fireman. You know, I think the Adams Place was unique in that it had a porch that went virtually around the house, and interesting gables and one Gothic Cupola (non functional). The Adams Place did not leave me with the same impressions, the concept of space and other impacts. Maybe it was enclosed with more trees and maybe I should have gone beyond the property lines to see the Piper Cub land and takeoff. Or Victor Weisskopf may have felt it better in his Knowledge and Wonder (1962)

"In man's brain the impressions from the outside are

not merely registered; they produce concepts and ideas. They are the imprint of the external world upon the human brain. Therefore, it is not surprising that, after a long period of searching and erring, some of the concepts and ideas in human thinking should have come gradually closer to the fundamental laws of this world...Nature, in the form of man, begins to recognize itself."

The great ideas have truly come from man close to nature and it nature is not too harsh man will reflect and see his own refection. From obscure places in the world have come the science of genetics, the miracles of the peanut, the harnessing of electricity, the development of writing and other Promethean secrets.

The Adams Place most likely was in Hart County because I remember Papa's walking ten miles to Hartwell to get medicine and ten miles back. If we were in Franklin County, surely Lavonia or Royston would be closer. I shall ask my oldest living sister about it. Maybe I can visit the area and see what remains. Like the other places, Adams will bring tears to my eyes.

When I was five, we moved to the Sam Sloan place, a significant influence and memory. The customary environs were there - thin soil with red visible in areas, house with customary front porch partially enclosed, back porch a few steps from the well platform, outbuildings including toilet and cotton house and beyond the barn the ubiquitous watershed and stream. Nature's new contribution was the flying squirrel which could not only climb and jump from limb to limb, but could also spread four legs, exposing a sail surface and could actually "fly" from one tree to another.

The Sam Sloan Place was a constant surprise and delight. I think that the owner had lived there himself. Although there was no electricity or plumbing, the house was a little above the average sharecropper shack. There was another clue to its history because at the barn shed (lean to) there was a disabled Model T! The Model T was also a new experience. My siblings and I drove the "T" to every place we knew about without leaving the barn. I can still feel the extraordinary steering wheel, the throttle, the brakes and the canopy frame on the old jalopy. This non-functional jalopy was the closest Papa ever got to owning an automobile until 1942 when we replaced our waterwheel for power source with an old Studebaker when the millpond washed away (or as my little sister described it "when the creek washed away").

Go south from Lavonia, Georgia (off Interstate 85 North) on Hwy. 17 and watch for a sign "Grady School Road." Turn west and you will not find the little brick two-room schoolhouse. Alas! The most famous school in the world was demolished. This would never have happened in certain parts of America or Europe. But it did happen. Grady School was only a half-mile from the Sam Sloan Place and proved to be the best start in education that a young sharecropper could have. The senior teacher there, Ms. W. from Lavonia, taught grades four, five and six. Her boarder, Ms. A. taught primer, second and third. I forget but it could be that primer was followed by "first." At any rate, my siblings had already "home-schooled" me so fortunately or unfortunately I was moved up a grade in the same room. I was only sixteen when I graduated from high school at Royston and my early departure is still a moot point.

Oh, Grady, where art thou today? In our day when it is imagined that pumping more and more money into education will improve the level of performance, let it be known that with good teachers and good students, success can be had in a pig pen. When I reflect on Abraham Lincoln, Richard B. Russell, Robert Byrd and other backwoods leaders, I get apoplectic when someone suggests that what our school system needs is "More Money." We still have good instructors but the lack of a good depression in our economy had disrupted the focus of our youth. They're sitting there like no-feather birds in the nest waiting for education to drop into their heads. I'll save some of this philosophy for later chapters when this leisurely, mild-mannered approach of mine starts to hit rough weather. Then your head will be bouncing off the fuselage and you'll pull at least three G's at times.

My memory of the Sam Sloan Place is extraordinary. We tend to remember the pleasant things such as a sweet, caring teacher like Ms. A. The only unpleasant memory was lending my rubber ball to the older students at Grady to play stickball and they would return it all pitted and disfigured. I got over that entirely.

New Franklin Christian Church (Disciples of Christ) is still there. There's also a sign on Hwy. 17 about a mile from "Grady School Road" which points the way to the church. I remember walking with the family toward Grady School, making a right turn down, then up to the New Franklin Road. One Sunday morning there was a tow truck pulling a Saturday night loss of control vehicle from the ditch. A very novel experience was explained to me then, which I now interpret as a DUI.

At New Franklin, too, were the "All Day Singing-dinner On The Grounds." I must say that the community DINNER was one occasion when I actually got enough to eat in my early years. One can readily see that the Sam Sloan Place offered great advantages to a barefoot towhead like me. Several years ago, I went to New Franklin Church to try to re-orient myself to Grady School and Sam Sloan. A good neighbor nearby the church finally convinced me I had a mirror image of my boyhood map and should turn on an unpaved road to the north rather than to the south. Sure enough, there was the Grady School place now occupied by a domestic dwelling and white fence and only another turn to the west and *voila*! There was the Sam Sloan Place. More memories began to flood in.

Let me tell you about another bonus which came to me at six years of age. I found a buddy who lived between Sam Sloan and Grady School on the Waters Place. He was seven, sophisticated and worldly wise. He was an expert hurler of rocks by hand or slingshot ("flip"). He knew everything about gender and geography; nevertheless, he was gentle and protective and vowed to beat up any older boys threatening me. We played in the field in good weather and in the barn loft and stables in bad weather. The barn loft was his undoing because while visiting relatives miles away, he was playing in the barn loft and upon retreating from angry wasps stepped back on a loose board which catapulted him through the hay loading window onto the ground and broke his neck. He did not survive. Mama heard the news before I did and she was very upset and sought me to reprimand me for my role in the tragedy because she thought that the accident happened just up the road at the Waters Place. This was my first acquaintance with death and the disappearance of an image which would never return.

When you read these anecdotes and impressions, you may call me for others if you wish. Otherwise, I will reduce the volume. I do not want to air my soul upon the unconcerned or the unwilling. Any Boy Scout can tell you that it's easier to help the oldsters across the street if they're willing to go. I do praise my Maker for giving me the sharecropper's experience. I shudder to think that I might have been the son of a wealthy urbanite and missed the proximity to nature, reality, the majority of humankind, and what the Spaniards call *semejante* or an identification with humanity. While other writers in their memories primarily relate events and incidents with actual names and places, I have, as far as possible, withheld the names of actual people so that they fall categorically into the scheme of things.

I hate to leave Sam Sloan. I wanted you to know that there were neighbors I remember. One of the neighbors had an automobile and worked somewhere in a neighboring town and came home every day at a predictable time. He had sons and one of them had gone up to the Waters Place and obtained a bucket of ripe figs. On his return, my sister and I trailed along with him. My sister, two and a half years my senior, was mischievous and begged him for a fig. He pretended to comply but purposefully dropped the fig and crushed it into the dirt road. This happened several times and my sister swore revenge. She did not know how to punish the son so she decided to punish the parents. The next day prior to the arrival of Mr. B. from his job, we went up the road toward Grady School and built a gravel and dirt traffic bump across the road. (This most likely was the first in America, however you can search "Speed Bumps" and see what you can hit.) Mr. B. told Papa soon after that he did not see the bump before he hit it and I might paraphrase it in modern aviation terms: "I rotated at 60 MPH, found myself in ground effect and landed with a ground loop." Papa announced the event categorically "wondering who did this prank" but I think he knew. My older sister nor I ever confessed.

Speaking of sisters, I should like to praise the eldest at this time. Anderson, South Carolina was about thirty miles distant across the great Savannah River. There was a Fair held there every year and she made arrangements to go by bus from Grady School and somehow against good judgment took me along. We certainly walked several miles during the Fair and upon returning to Grady, we began the half-mile to Sam Sloan. I was able to walk on my little legs about a hundred yards but the ache was too much and I begged for piggyback. The poor girl, herself tired, carried me the remainder of the way. I thought often of this act, not only getting me out of the state for the first time but the finishing touch of carrying Little Achy Legs the distance. When I cared for her in her final years, it was a pleasure to remember her kindness on my first "International Trip!"

Then there was the Estes Place. This was not a great move from Sam Sloan. The general environs included Poplar Springs Campground (Methodist), Nelm Wilson's Store at the Crossroads from Canon and Dawkins School. Cromer's Mill Creek was the watershed. Observe the pattern of the sharecropper's world. Really it was a decent place in spite of being watershed.

Dawkins School was my first traumatic social experience. The second and third grade teacher

(Freud blocks out her name from my memory) only shouted until her voice was raspy and harsh. She had some hang-ups too, because in her more somber moments advocated to us that we put oatmeal on our hands to prevent wrinkles. How many seven and ten year olds have wrinkles? My next oldest sister, mentioned before, and I trekked the two miles via the hypotenuse of a triangle, usually arriving wet or cold. One morning we couldn't make it but turned around in the bitter wind in our unlined coats and came back to the fire. We were teased a bit by the elders but we were welcomed home. How I survived the second grade and my sister the third grade was a mystery to me. Perhaps it was our good foundation in the language that allowed us to stumble through the math. We were absent a lot and our teacher was one of the truant officers that visited in our humble home and was very laudatory about us in the presence of our parents. If I were not so intimidated by the teacher, I believe I would've had a better experience with math throughout my career. I often quip (again Freudian-like) that I was bitten by a number when I was small and never recovered. In reality, I was "bitten" by a teacher and never fully recovered. Fortunately, in the Fall of '39, Papa arranged for a pickup converted to a bus to pick us up and transport us to Canon, which was almost as close as Dawkins. How strange it is to block unpleasantries out of the mind. I found out that all teachers are not compassionate to unlearned sharecropper kids.

There were beautiful events and atmospheres about the Estes watershed. First Son came home to visit from South Carolina. "Papa, why haven't you ordered the kids clothes from Sears-Roebuck?" I still remember - he took the catalog, peeled off the order blank, sat down and through his magic figured out quantity and size and posted the order in the mail. In a few days Rural Free Delivery mail delivered a package to the Estes Place. Second Son was not there at the time but the remainder of the family was. First Son soon returned to South Carolina. I remember that he would sit in a chair, extend his hands outward and one of us would sit on one hand and another on the other. He would lift his hands up and down. He was very strong. All the brothers were strong, able to dog ear a hundred pound bag of fertilizer and throw it on a wagon.

At the Estes Place Second Son also came home. He had interesting things called cigarettes. Papa used only smokeless tobacco and Third Son from the Rock rolled his own. Fascinated by the cigarettes I took one and a match and went down near the woods and started to smoke. Second Son saw me and started to give chase. I had a head start and disappeared into the woods, which I knew. One of my older sisters pleaded for my forgiveness and sought me out in the woods and guaranteed my safe return. Soon after that, I ended my smoking career when friends of Papa brought Cuban cigars over - long, green Cuban cigars. Papa saw me watching the event with interest and he said to me, "Son, would you like to try one of these?" I said "uh huh." After a couple of puffs I turned as green as the Cuban cigar, went to a secluded place and lost my cigar and my lunch! Don't tell me you can't give up tobacco.

Second Son was always surprising us by coming from Atlanta to visit. He was a likeable fellow with black hair, blue eyes and black brows. He could have doubled for William Holden, the actor. He took a special interest in a stray dog that had followed Papa and wagon from Canon. Papa would get out of the wagon and throw stones to drive the middle size dog back to his own home, but the dog, knowing God's will and his fate, persisted and came home with Papa. He had a good chest and teeth and was forever chewing and shaking objects. Second Son took the young dog down to the creek and introduced him to water moccasins. Dutifully, the dog caught and shook the snakes, shaking himself into a full-time career. At the Estes Place I forgave Second Son for whipping me when he caught me urinating across the road in *flagrante delicto*. How dare he exercise in *loco parentis!*

It just shows that love overcomes revenge even for a sharecropper kid. Besides, at the Adams Place I had already done a heroic act; after being missing for a few hours, I came home and reported that I had encountered a snake as large as the house, which had a small red tooth, and I stomped and killed it.

At seven years of age, one of my summer duties

was to make halters for the calves and tie them out or hold them for grazing. I found that calves and bovines don't have upper teeth but simply wrap their tongues around the grass and pull against the lower teeth. Equally fascinating was their ruminant characteristics. After grazing all day they would lie down, regurgitate the fermenting grass, and chew it for digestion. I learned that they employed two stomachs for this purpose, whereas chickens have a grinder (gizzard), which prepares the food for the intestines. In those eventful years of 1938 and 1939, I learned duties about the farm and felt proud to partner with Third Son from the Rock with my feeble efforts. I learned to run, too. We would be in the back field and Papa would say, "You're little and light - go to the barn and get a heel sweep for the cultivator or something else. Sometimes I would get the wrong implement so off to the errand again. I developed speed and strength, and by the time I played end in football, I could "truck" and catch with my hands.

We had a great wheat crop in 1939, and followed with no-till peas. When we harvested the peas we put posts in the ground, stretched a pole between the posts and hung the pea vines over the poles. It was great hay in my opinion so I was greatly disappointed that the cows didn't eat it. I felt that they were very ungrateful for the work we did.

Always a treat but a rare one was a visit to Nelm Wilson's Store. A stick of candy or an "all-day" sucker was a real accomplishment. Of course sugar led to teeth problems and Papa introduced us to frayed sassafras branch cuts and tooth powder. We had never had brushes before and the sassafras brushes tasted good. This did not solve all our dental problems but it was a good start.

In spite of psychologically depressing experiences with Dawkins School, the Estes Place leaves a somewhat comforting and tranquil memory. It was nestled between the plateau and watershed, the creek yielding "wash holes' for summer fun. In general we were insulated from the harshness of the Depression, visited by the older siblings and Papa was still young enough to participate with Third Son on the watershed. You may weary of "watershed" but I must remind you that on the plateaus of South Georgia, the valley of the Tennessee River in North Alabama, sharecroppers certainly had a different experience. Watershed sharecroppers were most likely "worse off" than the others.

At the Estes Place I also became acquainted with the much maligned and little understood Georgia penal system, popularly called "Chain Gang" who wore the horizontal referee stripes. Wooden bridges were common in North Georgia and the creek that ran near the Estes Place had a wooden bridge occasionally needing replacement. The Chain Gang arrived to make the repairs, and I as "wide-eyed as a cat in front of a new barn door" (a German expression I read in Simplicissimus by Von Grimmelshausen), perched on an embankment by the bridge and watched two black inmates driving iron bars into the ground, one holding the iron and the other swinging a sixteen pound hammer. "What if he misses?" I thought worriedly. The muscular man holding the bar perceived my concern and while the swinger was taking a brief break said "He don't miss cuz my turn to swing is coming." They seemed amused at the little towhead boy on the bank and I, never reluctant to converse with strangers, urged them to keep talking. Even the guard with a shotgun wasn't too uptight about the situation and conversed with me also. This initial experience has helped me throughout life to differentiate between prisoners who were at the wrong place at the wrong time and those who are pathologically hardened and have an underdeveloped hypothalamus.

Maybe due to my aging and maturation at the Estes Place, I began to develop a portent for the future, sensing that we were entering a new phase of life. And truly this happened, for our next move was to the Parham Place at Franklin Springs, formerly a spa and vacation place now populated primarily by Pentecostals, boasting a junior college, a printing press and a post office.

The end of our sharecropping experience came to a close at the Parham Place. Papa had contracted with the widow Parham to sharecrop or tenant the area just south of Franklin Springs. The "farm" boasted a typical sharecropper house with partially enclosed front porch, back porch with washstand, a barn near the creek and a storage outbuilding. The exciting addition to the spread was a real water-powered corn mill and a syrup mill and of course a millpond or reservoir.

Then there was Franklin Springs. Before I was born, Papa and family had lived behind Dixie Dale or at that time behind Center School where one of my sisters was born. Prominent and on tourist maps today is Victoria Bryant State Park built near the shoals of Cromer's Mill Creek where we used to grapple for fish under the rocks, praying that we would not pull our a water moccasin. Third Son mentioned that there was a skating rink at the "Springs" also. In fact, Franklin Springs was so famous that saying "Springs" would immediately identify the place and it was named even before Royston.

Not long after we moved there, J. H., a youth, stopped by our house on his way south and gave us some religious literature (tracts) printed by the Advocate Press. We had never had an experience like that. Eventually I was to spend some time at the press then located near the springs but now located on the plateau on Hwy. 29. I was fascinated by the linotype printing and the melting pot for melting down the "babbit" to form more set printing. Of course we fell for the old trick of looking into the water between two rows of type and the criminal typesetter would shove the rows together and we would catch the water in the face. We never made the same mistake twice because we were ever busy making new ones. However, none of us fell for "snipe hunting" whose trick was universally known.

We had moved to Franklin Springs very near the Christmas of '39, the year of the big snow and I've told you how Third Son dealt with the lack of food by catching about twenty rabbits. Also, we were extra careful not to burn the house down because there are very few things more tragic than the loss of a sharecroppers home. No insurance and no backup paints a dismal picture. Even one of the founding fathers saw the possibilities which might result from signing the Declaration of Independence and qualified his objections by saying "Dear Friends, one must not burn his house down in December."

A real bonus for arriving near Christmastime was that my contemporaries were home for Christmas vacation and the W. boys from Hwy. 29 were riding their mules and stopped at the creek to water them. They initiated conversation and I found out that I would be a classmate to one of them and we remained friends throughout the school experience at Royston and I regard him as a friend today even though I have not seen him since high school days.

The Ws were a large family, even larger than ours, so we had the same temperament and predilection to sharing and unselfishness. The father was a hard taskmaster and left the children little time for home study ("homework") so I spent many nights by lamplight studying with my contemporaries. They credited me with their graduating but I must say in all honesty, that they were smarter than I, and what I learned passively and slowly, they learned aggressively and quickly.

I guess - in fact I know - we differed substantially and culturally from the Springs folks but we managed some sort of symbiosis and intercultural co-existence. We were forever referred to as "the people down on the creek." About twenty years ago, our college coach in Alabama wanted to invite an athlete from Emmanuel College to visit us. I flew my plane to the Franklin County Airport to pick him up. I told his coach I had family in Franklin Springs and after describing their habitation he said, "Oh, you're from the family 'down on the creek'."

I did not accept all the people at Franklin Springs *Carte Blanche*. I really admired several of the older Pentecostals such as Old Man D. and Granny J. They prayed for themselves and for others, and were very genuine converts. Old man D. farmed his "patch" and sold his butterbeans and other vegetables in Royston. Then there was the philosopher and artist J. K. What a Renaissance Man! My sister still has J. K.'s sketch for our old farmhouse, barn and mill. He gave a eulogy at Third Son's funeral and I still weep when I think about it.

Reflecting upon Franklin Springs, I remember a great number I admired and now treasure the memory. What was really eerie in a way in the early 40s were the night prayers emanation from the cemetery and the hills. As old Grandpa D. said years after 1940 "We

106

just don't pray and shout enough anymore: we're getting too worldly." I agree, Old Man. ("Old Man" or "Viejo" in Spanish are words of respect.)

When I point my index finger in reprimand, at least three fingers are pointed back at me. I'm very certain that I was not a model of demeanor or decorum either. This is not a confessional but I wish I had worked more on the farm and spent less time in the Springs. I did work very hard during the war, when Third Son was in the military and during Second Son's brief return to the farm for spring planting and summer cultivation. Thereafter he joined the Navy, went to San Diego, thence to the Pacific. I did work hard enough and long enough to know what I have expressed previously: No one can make a living in a rock pile unless one finds gold.

The Parham Place experience in a way is almost synonymous with Franklin Springs, one of the differences being that in 1940, First Son was killed in an auto accident and Papa prudently bought the Parham Place with the life insurance money. We then became poor farmers rather than poor sharecroppers. Widow Parham was very liberal in the financial settlement and I thank her in retrospect.

Most sharecropping ended during WWII and the immediate aftermath. As the old song says, "How ya gonna keep 'em down on the farm after they've seen Paree?" Well, Third Son came back to the farm but modified his profession by participating in Veterans programs of welding, livestock raising and cover crops. Gone were the days of subsistence survival on the Parham Place as well as thousands of other "Places" in the nation. Of course, thousands of "Places" were disappearing everywhere. Because of the great number of Mississippi sharecroppers (especially blacks) migrating to Chicago, etc., sociologists give more attention to that page of Greyhound and Train transhumance. The Robert Taylor Apartments and other complexes have stories of their own and one can find a lot of film, facts and fiction on the subject. I saw a lot of the projects in 1950 when I hitched through Illinois from Georgia to get to Wisconsin to work in the automotive industry. The Great Depression had moved a number of us around the nation during the "Remedy" programs such as construction of the Hoover Dam, the Civilian Conservation Corp, oil exploration and gas pipelines in Louisiana and Texas, the opening of the overseas highway from Miami to Key West, further land speculation in Florida, and Florida's climate which attracted many to the potentials of paper mills and truck farming promoted by both federal and state agencies. The Parham Place, then, was not the only institution ready to be dismantled. Yes, the Parham Place and Franklin Springs were only a small part of the nation affected by changes brought about by World War II. Yet they surely were affected less because the area did not factor prominently in the cotton market to begin with. This fits my concept of Royston and the environs as playing a role primarily in the horizontal spread of cotton after the Civil War.

World War II speeded up vertical production in just about every area of life, fully adopting the Westinghouse and Ford Motor Company's assembly and mass production. The necessity of winning the war amplified and accelerated all facets of life. The ultimate effects of all of this are now beginning to be seen. Consumerism has been the benchmark and percentage of unemployment represents the number employable but does not show the social equation of revealing the great number who should NOT be employed. Unlike quiet Franklin Springs, we have degenerated from one parent working outside the home to two parents working outside the home, from poor land being used for farming to rich, arable earth being used for airfields, factories, shopping centers, miracle miles, subdivisions - all to keep up mad consumerism, the "haftahavits" which we really don't "havtahav." During the Great Depression and deflation, twenty-five percent were unemployed; during a possible Great Depression in the future, we'll be looking at seventy-five percent. Marginal jobs were lost during the Depression. Marginal jobs will be lost in such an event today, and there are millions of marginal jobs. Even in Royston and environs, few people are doing what their parents and grandparents did and close scrutiny will not call it "progress." "Activity" and "Progress" may be mutually exclusive and have always been debatable and difficult to distinguish. As Ed Sullivan told Elvis Presley, "Don't just do something: Stand there."

THE GRAND DEPRESSION
The Sharecropper Perspective

A sharecropper's son writes to his folks from the Civilian Conservation Corp in Clayton, Georgia in the Blue Ridge Mountains:

Clayton, GeorgiaAug. 5, 1934
Dear Folks,
I wrote a letter to you the day I arrived and I haven't heard from you yet. I don't know whether you got it or not. I am still liking the camp (fine?) at Lake Burton. It is 20 miles west of Clayton. I will begin work Wed. six hours per day. I am getting along fine gaining more beef everyday, sleeping like a log and eating like a hog. Write me whether you got my letter or not.BillClayton, Ga.Camp F-10

P. S. They are having a festival up here at the Camp and at the lake all the best swimmers and high divers in the south are up here. It is from the 5th to the 12th. We will have about 7 or 8 hundred visitors here all the week. This is a big week. I have already been issued about $60 dollars worth of clothes. It is pretty lonesome up here in the sticks. The sun don't rise until about 10. I will come home about 3rd Sunday. I can come home any weekend with C. D. Stovall who lives at Hartwell. He is a teacher up here. I am taking typing, first aid, English and commercial arithmetic.

And a postcard from the same lad July I, 1938 from Atlanta, GA:

Hello Folks,
I have a job waiting on me in Baton Rouge, La. Fred Hyde got it for me. 50cents per hour, 60 hours a week. I don't want to lose time hitchhiking. If you can wire me about $15 quick as you get this card because I want to get gone. Pay you back soon as I can make it.

Write more next time.
Bill H.
771 Edgewood Ave.

Apparently Bill made it to Baton Rouge and then on to Houston for he writes from Houston, Texas on September 26, 1938:

I am in Houston, Texas, got in this afternoon. The job doesn't start until 15th of October. I will work in Baytown, Texas. I have no address yet, will write again.

Bill

The Above is the correspondence of a sharecropper using that great medium of the United States of America - Rural Free Delivery. The cost was very minimal. Most countries in the world today do not have rural delivery. I have seen more shrines than mailboxes in Latin America along the back roads. The sharecropper's son wrote hurriedly, yet his style and literacy is better than that of most youth of today.

The title "Grand Depression" describes my concept of the era. It was an era of reflection, discipline and a reevaluation of the Teens and Twenties of our nation. Following World War II the nation protested against President Wilson's American ideals, his determination to structure the League of Nations and to take a leadership role in World Affairs. The nation wanted to be grasshoppers (not ants) and twiddle to their own affairs. Rebels drank in cabarets, drank bootleg gin, poked fun at "normal" Americans in novels and plays.

Of course there were conservatives, prohibitionists and reformers during the Twenties, but they could not stem the tide of carefree living, flagrant speculation in the stock market, unusual tariffs to protest American business and thumbed nose to the rest of the world. "Ain't we got fun?" a song as well as an attitude pervaded the American scene. Sound familiar? In 1928, one of the most remarkable men in U. S. History became President - Herbert Clark Hoover. To protect the American farmer he asked Congress for a protective agricultural tariff. Congress broadened it to a more comprehensive tariff, which defeated the purpose originally intended. The grasshoppers thought that not only was prosperity great but it was going to get better. Conservatives recognized that the seeds of depression were already sown but no one listened. Foreign governments were already losing faith in the American policies.

Much greater economists and historians than I have enumerated and discussed the causes of the Great Depression. Causes and cures often are obscured by the fog of blame. It was very convenient to blame the Hoover Administration rather than assess the responsibility of business and financial institutions. Should the phenomena of Depression rear its frightening head today, the first inclination would be to blame the President and Administration and demand that they fix it. But who fixes it? It is the working class, the sharecroppers and tenant farmers, the engineers, the mechanics, and in general those who drain to make sacrifices rather than to pass the blame on to the government. The government can do only so much: it is the character and resolve of the people who make it happen. I read in the Bible (Isaiah?) "KEMO AM, KEMO KOHEN" ("Like People, Like Priest"). I thought they had gotten it backwards: the priest will be like the people? I have found this to be true in America. The people will elect a good president but will wheedle him down to their standards. People refuse to change until significant conditions and events cause them to change. Tragically, something like the Grand Depression has to occur to change us. Planned recessions may be the disciplinary key to preventing total collapse.

In the Grand Depression, the population was smaller, significantly rural, and in general possessed a work ethic. If the economy has to be maintained by population growth there will come a point when "square" people will exceed the viable "square miles" of the nation. A more practical concept than consumerism has to be developed. At least America, which played a leading role in the worldwide Depression, "bit the bullet" until the economy could be remedied. Some nations turned to Hitler and Tojo.

The generation of the Twenties that "roared", speculated, "flapped", and speculated, plunged my generation into poverty, hunger and hopelessness. The roof caved in and the bottom fell out. White-collar employees everywhere lost their positions and turned to various pursuits to sustain themselves as they marched through the land with holes in their shoes. Sharecroppers clung to their cropping and barely survived. Ty Cobb had already quit baseball and baseball salaries were reduced, but baseball continued to be a national pastime. Ten-cent admission to movies was very popular to take the mind off reality. America dug in.

Germany embraced socialism (NAZI), and Italy fascism. The Nazis began to isolate and plan the extinction of Jewish Germans. Russia kept exporting the grain of the Ukrainians to put on a showy front while the Ukrainians starved by the hundreds of thousands, many eating the horses and dogs. Children were not safe on the streets. There was so much sentiment in Russia against the Stalinists that if the Germans had been smart they could've gone in as saviors rather than brutal conquerors.

The engines and cogs of worldwide economies had ground to a halt, one shutdown following another. Saudi Arabia received few pilgrims in Mecca because of the worldwide depression. Pilgrims just didn't have travel funds; the Saudi coffers were empty. In 1932, the Saudis invited the Americans (CASOC or California Standard Oil Co.) to explore for oil in Eastern Arabia. The Brits had been in Iran and Bahrain already. Wild Catters from Texas and Oklahoma came, chewing their tobacco and spitting dust. Eventually, in 1938, CASOC produced a gusher at Dhamman. Saudi Arabia began, due to worldwide depression, to play a major and irreversible role in global political economies. Yes Children, connections in history are very interesting. "For want of a nail a horseshoe was lost, for want of a horseshoe, a horse was lost, for want of a horse, a kingdom was lost." The Civil War created a dependence on Egyptian cotton, etc.

The U. S. participation in World War I exaggerated, puffed up the image of America. These tall, pioneer-hardened youth about Ty Cobb's age marched into France with "La Fayette, the Yanks are coming" and "we won't be back 'til it's over over there!" European monarchs and secretaries of state were not so disposed to recognize the premature impact of the Yanks as the people were. Remember the great crowds at La Bourget when the six foot four inch Charles Lindbergh landed? If the leaders of France and Britain had listened to President Wilson and the reports of the King Crane Commission, the Middle East (or so called Near East in Britain) would certainly have begun Arab States autonomy much sooner than World War II. But hindsight is still very good.

So... with the U. S. financial collapse in 1929, the Dominoes fell over worldwide. This should not have been the case yet the U. S.' premature giant reputation in the world gave us an undeserved importance. Of course there was our success against the Kaiser, the completion of the Panama Canal abandoned by the French, the liberation of Cuba and the Philippines, the presence of our shipping industry around the world and our general display of muscles, yet these alone should not have caused the rest of the world to follow our collapse.

Then there were some insidious practices in the U. S. that were factors in the Grand Depression. We had greedily plowed too wide and too deep in the great prairies from Texas to Canada and we paid dearly for the abuse. The Depression was also the Dust Bowl and "Grapes of Wrath" sown by our farmers on the Great Prairies. It is really a miracle that the U. S. survived its own practices of self-destruction. The plows went too wide and too deep on the prairies, and the plows should never have come to Royston and the Georgia Piedmont. What was blowing away on the Prairies was washing away in Royston. "Gully" was a word in everyone's vocabulary.

Texas, Oklahoma and Kansas began to look more

like Iraq and Saudi Arabia than the roaming area of the buffalo where only the tracks of wagon trains should have been visible. Third Son told me about the dust. He said that when the west wind blew he could hardly see to plow because of the Oklahoma dust. Even in 1953 when I lived in Dallas, dust storms created low visibility and dirty rain.

Yet the Midwest and especially the lakes area - Minnesota, Wisconsin, Michigan, Ohio, etc... still produced a lot and the Depression was still not a case of lack of production but a case of poor distribution. The tragic case of wholesale slaughter of pigs and calves to bring up the price of meat failed to bring up the price. Then the transhumanance of the unemployed and dust bowl victims added its own chapter to the Depression.

Now children, you can find tons of information in books and on the Internet about the Great Depression, but as your old Grandpa, I've got to alert you to the Grand Depression. Underneath the cloud of dust, great engineering in automobiles, aviation and assembly production was quietly and efficiently doing its job. Henry Ford had already started the "continuous casting" process of steel in 1920 (which the Japanese "discovered" in 1980), which by 1942, in combination with assembly, was to overwhelm the equally great and sometimes superior war machines of Germany and Japan.

The main industries belied the unemployment, natural disasters and the hurried socio-economic remedies of the FDR Era. World War II was already being discussed in the Sam Sloan and Estes Places by First Son and Papa in 1937, '38, '39. Had not the Depression industries worked patiently and diligently in research and development, the Free World would've been in an unfortunate predicament to retaliate against the aggression in several theatres of war.

An interesting anecdote involving Clyde Barrow (Bonnie and Clyde), a sort of cult hero of the anti-establishmentarians, ironically synthesized the success of the Depression years. He wrote Henry Ford, thanking Ford for the development of the V-8 engine, which enabled Barrow to elude the police time and time again.

The foregoing demonstrates the elasticity of America's working people. Their efforts paid off because when the war was engaged, military vehicles were coming off the lines every minute, bombers every hour and ships every week. Abraham Lincoln's attitude prevailed during the Depression.

"Mr. Lincoln, why do you continue to read those books and study so much?"

"Sir, I shall continue to study: Some day my country may have need of me."

And the country did.

Religion (*religere* "to bind back") starts man back toward his maker. Philosophy helps him understand the necessity and beauty of it all. The NAZIS had no intention to self-examine: they simply supported a mustached Austrian who was turned down twice by the Munich School of Art (I'll never forgive those "Holier Than Thou" administrators), and called forth the trumpets of Wagner and the philosophy of Nordic Supermen. What was originally thought to be the philosophy of Friedrich Nietzsche. Now, since the fall of the Berlin Wall, we have evidence formerly held by the Russians, which reveals that it was Friedrich's philosophy seriously tampered with by Elizabeth, Friedrich's sister and Hitler's "Grand Lady of Weimar." The forgoing is also a typical German sentence in length and complexity.

Pardon an overview and repetition of the Grand Depression. The sharecroppers are still sharecropping. Not much has changed from the Twenties except for deflation in the price of cotton. Deflation in other areas did equalize the problem somewhat. In Georgia, the free textbook provision under Governor E. D. Rivers gave the sharecropper youngsters the best opportunity to learn. I have known very few sharecroppers, including the black sharecroppers, who were illiterate.

It is a testimony to the availability of schools, good teachers, respectful youngsters and free education that learning was pervasive. I hear people today say, "We've just got to put more money into public schools!" Bah, humbug! I'm more inclined to say, "We've got to put more good students into public schools!" As Art Buchwald parodied Gov. Lester Maddox of Georgia, "We're not going to have better prisons in Georgia until we get a better class of prisoners!"

Another broad perspective for the Depression is the movement of people. The Okies were a new Oregon Trail but this time to California. Many oil and gas workers, including sharecroppers, went to Louisiana and Texan and some to Saudi Arabia. Former white-collar workers and many blue-collar workers rode the freight trains and lined up at soup lines and relief agencies. Late in the Depression and at the beginning of war conflict in Europe, sharecroppers by the thousands hit the bus and train trail to Chicago and Cleveland. Joe Louis, the boxer, had been part of an earlier migration from Alabama to Detroit where he began his boxing career in 1934.

The movement from rural to urban and then back to sub-urbia and eventually to pen-urbia (almost rural again!) was a phenomenon of the war years and the aftermath. Underneath all of the movement, there was the solid continuation of the automotive ("the old LaSalle ran great"), aviation, tool and die manufacturers (Cincinnati, Ohio was virtually depression proof) and basic appliances (remember the refrigerator with the compressor on top?)

In danger of repeating myself, I must reiterate: people worked ten hours a day during the Depression to earn a livelihood. They had to improvise, entertain themselves and were rarely bored. Now we work (both parents) outside the home twenty hours a day to pay for our laborsaving devices, we don't know how to improvise or entertain ourselves, and we neglect to love and educate our children. Should I say, "Bring on a Depression!" Or, remembering that we no longer have the sharecropper survival instinct say "O Great Spirit, be merciful to us."?

WORLD WAR II

"A time for war and a time for peace."
(Hebrew Bible Ecclesiastes 3:8)

I don't know when World War II began. Thucydides, the great Greek historian, made the distinction clear between the cause of war and the occasion (event) of war. The cause of WWII may go back two centuries when the northern Europeans took the baton of the accomplishments of the Arabs and the Renaissance and carried it to new heights of technology and power of the Nordics and Prussians described by Friedrich Nietzsche.

Some believe that WWII began in effect following the defeat of Germany and the limitations put upon Germany by the Treaty of Versailles. Although never implemented completely, the Germans felt that the Treaty (1920) imposed harsh reparations (about $33 billion) on them, yet the reparations were never collected from Germany.

Perhaps the Germans were propagandized into believing that their Depression was caused by the western nations, and used military buildup as a way to restore the economy. The science of propaganda, historically common, was honed to a frightening efficiency by Hitler and his henchmen. When Franklin Delano Roosevelt became President in 1933, Hitler was appointed Chancellor of Germany by Hindenburg. In 1934, Hindenburg died and Adolph

Hitler declared himself der Fuhrer (the Leader) of Germany. Then began the most sinister, the most destructive, the most terrible epoch of history known to mankind.

Adolph Hitler was a name I would come to know in the sharecropper's shack, especially as the winds of war began to blow the clouds toward the inevitable horror. Papa and First Son no longer argue over "Who made God?" Papa, in his unconscious Aristotelianism, believed humbly that to say that it was "God who made God" was "Infinite Regression" (this term he did not use!), and one cannot go beyond the Creator. So the two began to talk about an impending war, and my big ears took in everything while my heart sank.

I learned later that Japan had invaded Manchuria in 1937 and by December 1938 controlled China's main ports, industry and rails. (Understand that the details of these matters did not reach the Sam Sloan or the Estes Places but their essence did.) Except for a brief period in the 1920s, militarism was supreme in Japan and aggression was pronounced. Most of the western world just hoped that this aggression would truncate itself. Britain and the U. S. hoped a lot in those days and hope was primarily our greatest commodity.

Kingdoms fell to the dictators who built up armies and armaments. The eventual winners of the war were the last to build and mobilize. The U. S. had only 250,000 in the military but before the end of the war, had over 10 million in uniform. We were not prepared to think about war, let alone prepared for war. I preferred that Papa and First Son would discuss theology when the lad came home from Depression jobs, but the talks became more centered around the rumblings in Europe. Maybe I told you that First Son took the stance of Charles Lindberg who favored a defensive war and even quipped that Argentina was beginning to look very attractive.

Yet, the conflict in Spain and the increased activity of Papa's "Red Shirts" (whoever they were) increased my anxiety. Some psychologists say that we should protect our children from these serious and dire events but I disagree. Children should know what's out there and how many people are dying so that they can live. When these children grow up they will not live in fools' paradise, believing that they can appease these evil tyrants around the world who only have a "will to power" and not a "will to do good." The difference between Hitler and Emanuel Kant is antipodal. Every generation has to put down this evil and remember the words of George Washington, "To be prepared for war is one of the most effectual means of preserving peace." (First Annual Address, January 8, 1790).

I don't know the psychological damage of rumors of war, but it's quite evident among those who survived Buchenwald, Bergen-Belsen and Dachau. Maybe it's better that we toughen up while we're young, and avoid the mental pulled muscle and atrophy of adulthood. "The price of liberty is eternal vigilance." Eternal vigilance is tough but immeasurably better than the trauma of surprise and regret.

I have always liked the Brits. I liked British literature, British speech, British history, Robin Hood, Bloodless Revolutions and *ad infinitum*. Even though I suspect black-haired, black brows, and blue-eyed Papa was an "Irishman" and told humorous stories about Pat and Mike, I think Papa liked the Brits too.

I shall probably not forgive the yeomen of this country for the essence of the first ten amendments to the Constitution of the U. S. I debated this in college because my contention is that the so-called Bill of Rights is just a reactionary grocery list against British occupation, the Trojan Horse of our defeat. We should start with number eleven because the first ten seriously limit self-government. You lawyers out there, "put this in your pipe and smoke it!"

Now back to the War... When Hitler invaded Britain, his defeat and the end of the war was predictable. Britain always wins one battle - the last. Our ties with Britain are strong either in spite of or because of our struggle to gain independence from them. I suppose it may be because of our separation from them by a smaller ocean and "a common language!" Britain knew that we would be coming. We have never had the same relation with France although many things "French" have permeated out culture (including language) and our way of life. Churchill expresses the flip side of our relation with the French best "When I warned [the French] that

Britain would fight on alone whatever they did, their generals told their prime minister and his divided cabinet, 'In three weeks England will have her neck wrung like a chicken.' Some chicken! Some neck!"

Getting war-toughened was no problem for us children. We already knew hunger, exposure, sharing and sacrifice. We used, re-used and recycled. In 1942, our teacher suggested that we see a documentary at our local theater. It was a patriotic, emotional film (newsreel) filmed in Russia. After Britain regained the skies over their country, Hitler ill advisedly attacked Russia. After seeing the newsreel, my classmates and I were in awe of the Russian resistance. Instead of massing their troops at the border as Poland and Czechoslovakia had done, the Russians confronted them with a longitudinal line at the border, let the Germans break through soon to encounter another line, and another line all the way to Leningrad and to Moscow. The Russians were always on the Germans' flanks and delaying their advance while crack infantry divisions in white snow gear were being brought in from Siberia to confront the advancing Germans.

N. B., the classmate I referred to, lived on Campbell Ridge Road. He was ten years of age also. He rode his bicycle in from Campbell Ridge Road to Royston, and I walked in from Franklin Springs. After the newsreel, we rode double on his bike back to Campbell Ridge, not talking but reflecting on the sinister war and the awesome Russians. I have felt a kinship with the Russian people to this day. Two years ago I came across the same newsreel and I was surprised to discover how much of the reel I remembered.

Russia lost more people to the War than anyone else, not only because of Hitler but also because of the evil dictator Stalin. He "got religion" during the War. Betrayed by Hitler who broke their pact, Stalin turned to The Russian Orthodox Church to rally the people's support. If the iron head Germans had advanced as liberators rather then conquerors, the Russian people would have welcomed them. There's a considerable problem when one rules with an iron *head* rather than an iron *hand*.

During the War, my education (especially in geography and military science) grew like kudzu. A village paper route of the *Atlanta Constitution* opened up and I fell heir to it. I didn't have many customers, neither did I make a lot of money but I saved a paper each day so that I could keep up with current events, especially the theatres of war... North Africa, Britain, Germany, the Pacific and China. Son Two and Son Three were in the military and Little Brother read and wrote using a great number of 3-cent stamps.   T h e World War was everybody's war. Children saved for the war effort. Women went to work in the factories. Roosevelt's "Arsenal of Democracy" took on legs, wheels and wings as our own armies took the arsenal with them as opposed to shipping the arsenal to our allies. There was a somberness among us fourth, fifth, and sixth graders as the war intensified and turning points emerged. There were cheers and tears when Ms. R. announced our great victory at Midway in the Pacific. Americans were finding the value of propaganda to rally the citizenry. As we learned after the War, there was much truth about the atrocities committed by the Japanese and Germans. We learned about the horrible holocaust against the Jewish and Polish citizens.

This was the Great War. I have witnessed the Korean, Vietnam and Gulf Wars in which men and women fought and died yet for nobility of cause. This was the Great War. In the Great War we didn't have the U. N. fouling us up. We youngsters played war with homemade weapons and there were no injuries. It was difficult to convince your buddy, now a *pro tem* "enemy" that he was dead. "You're DEAD." "No, I'm not, you missed!" Anyway, we didn't do a lot of this because I was Papa's best source of human labor on the Piedmont "patches" of cotton, corn and sorghum. Some of my buddies were also strapped to the soil, but others weren't, so Sunday afternoon rivaled the Battle of North Africa on our little farm. I remember how amused Papa was by our tactics and strategy.

Papa wouldn't have been amused at our spying and surveillance. The local college hired an Asian cook - he was perhaps Filipino, Malaysian or Balinese, but we boys, of course, presumed he was Japanese. His radio, which we presumed to be short wave, blared at night and we could hear his voice from fifty yards away near a student dorm. Of course, he was sending strategic information (who could imagine such in Franklin Springs!) to Japan's Intelligence Bureau. This sounds ridiculous, but in retrospect it shows our complete patriotism for the survival of the Free World. But don't laugh! Hearsay indicates that an Emmanuel College Cook was discovered to be one of "America's Most Wanted" some years back. He had been a good employee for ten years!

One of the events of all times was the three-day movement of troops from Fort Benning, Georgia to maneuver with Fort Bragg or Camp Lejuene, North Carolina on U. S. Highway 29. Day and night the convoy rolled on the "wha, wha, wha," of the trucks over the concrete with the expansion grooves voicing "spat, spat, spat." Fuel for civilians was rationed anyway, so there was little to no domestic traffic on the roads. We thrilled to the outrider motorcyclists who leaned forty-five degrees to the left and then to the right to pass communications for miles at a time.

All the olive drab and ruddy soldiers, the Depression lads who were now well fed and well exercised, threw paper notes to way-siders, ostensibly inviting correspondence by offering name and address. Occasionally, the convoy would stop so that the main stream could work around an obstacle or eat rations and refresh. Brothers Two and Three were already in the military, and we wondered where they were and how they were faring. These soldiers on maneuvers were also our brothers, and tears came as we wondered where these young soldiers would be a year from now. Would they be marching forward or lying bleeding or dead on the fields of Africa, Europe or Asia?

Soon Highway 29 would be quiet again with only an occasional motor hum or a thump of the expansion creases. We youngsters vowed to join the men in Olive drab or Navy blues before very long. But fortunately, our brave men and women, backed up at home by equally brave and sacrificing folk, were able to bring the dictators to the Surrender Table and peace was gained at least for a few years. Free people have a history of winning wars and losing peace. It is so difficult to maintain the pace of war and have enough energy left to secure the peace.

"When the lights come on again, all over the world, and the boys come home again all over the world..."

We sang this over-and-over again and at that time remembered all the lyrics. Nights were long in the winter and I usually awoke hours before dawn, and would lie there and think about global matters. The war would take all trivial matters out of our minds and I imagined that Mama was awake also, thinking about her first-born lost to a drunken driver and her other sons in harm's way.

When Third Son from the Rock came home on furlough, I followed him around like a puppy dog, but of course, he wouldn't let me go into town with him at night. He would come in late and put his cold feet into my warm back, but I didn't mind. That's my brother. We found some transportation and took him back to catch a train in Atlanta. I can still see him walking reluctantly toward the station, saluting an officer on the sidewalk and then disappearing into the terminal. I knew he had tears because I did. It somehow took away the joy of my first trip to Atlanta and of stopping en route on U. S. Highway 78 to get a view of God's marvel, Stone Mountain.

I think it was former Governor of Alabama, George Wallace, who remarked about the cultural, economic and social revolution brought about by the war: "Yankees have come South, Southerners have gone North, cotton has gone West, and cattle have come East." Truly we were in "The end of the world as we knew it" ("TEOTWAWKI") since '39. The South abounded in military camps and many young men from other regions married Southern ladies. People who were feuding and stingy now shouldered together to produce every necessity of our lads and lassies in uniform. Women working outside the home started a trend that has grown to this day - an agrarian society became industrial and technical. Vertical production (more per acre, cow, factory) had replaced horizontal production. Enlightened people grieved that the Great Depression had virtually stopped immigration and we later found out that potential immigrants such as Jews and Polish nationals were slaughtered by the dictators.

Sensing the end of the War, commerce began to plan for overwhelming consumer goods to start hitting the market. No rational attempt to bring surplus vehicles was evident, for thousands upon thousands of vehicles were dumped into the Pacific Ocean. Deprivation during the War created a hunger for goods and there would enter the language a familiar word "disposable" to replace our heroes who were "expendable." Consumerism became a religion and waste a doctrine, and prodigals became heroes, so by 1965, thrift and conservation were cardinal sins. Woe to us if we allow our real heroes to die in vain. I welcome every shrine, museum and gathering of our veterans from the big war. As the Good Book says, "If I forget thee, O Jerusalem, let my right hand forget [its cunning]." The ancients knew something about the sub-station muscle, nerve and sinew memory that neurosurgeons are researching so diligently now especially since Christopher Reeve's case gained national attention. We need to memorize the heroics of our Veterans so that celebrations are automatic. It grieves me to see July 4th and Veterans' Day turned into Epicurean activities.

"Freedom Isn't Free" is a difficult concept for us Americans to understand and implement. Somebody has to pay. If we are not personally acquainted or connected with the ones who paid for our freedom, the concept is even more remote. Generations following the war generation tend to be less disciplined and pampered, especially in Consumerism. We cannot remember what we never knew and we cannot forget those traumas and ordeals that we knew very well. If we cannot forget the Alamo, the Maine and the Trail of Tears, how can we forget the Big War and its numerous "Forget Me Nots?" One of the shortcomings of our republic is that we do not have a monolithic epic tradition and the past is celebrated in multi-tenuous manners. Yet on the other hand, our diversity has its merits, for we can come together in a crisis. As an American, I am personally embarrassed that we require a depression or a crisis to activate our energies and resources (including patriotism). As I stated earlier, we win the war and lose the peace. In 1865, the Union won the war and with the death of Lincoln, the exploiters ("carpet-baggers") and opportunists lost the peace while the South almost starved. Little wonder that Tyrus Raymond Cobb grew up so tough.

The Big War (WWI was not the BIG WAR) still haunts me. I became acquainted with Incarnate Evil. The "Goose step" and pounding boots still resonate in my subconscious. The sinister "U-Boat" (German "unterseeboot") sank 400 ships from Nova Scotia to Argentina without resistance before we fought back. They even sank one in the Jacksonville, Florida harbor, not to mention the bloodbaths and destruction of our shipping in New Jersey, Coney Island and the Connecticut River. I have learned from my contact with the Civil Air Patrol that in turn the little Piper Cubs dropped 15 lb. bombs and managed to sink seven U-Boats. Once we found out the rules of engagement, we went after the U-Boats with destroyers and torpedo planes, and many U-Boats now lie on the ocean floor, sacrificed by the mustached Adolph Hitler who failed to be admitted to the Vienna School of Art.

Until my dying day the War will haunt my memory and emotions. I hope that my readers will ascertain the causes of the war and dwell on them, and treat the events of war as the natural consequences of cause. I am indebted to the great Greek historian Thucydides (c. 455-400 B. C.) who showed me the difference between cause and occasion, between a wide-angle comprehensive view and a narrow focus (often biased and erroneous) on the mere events of War. Thucydides was the first scientific historian. His predecessor, Herodotus, was not scientific: Herodotus was a collector of tales, myths, legends and provincial concepts. Nevertheless, he made valuable contributions to cultures and geography. Quite candidly, I am more like Herodotus than Thucydides, yet I strive to be more like Thucydides.

We Americans are much like the Greeks. We love athletics, adventure, nice things, and we love to talk. Of course, Greek names are different and "philosophy" scares high school students to death, but the Greeks, in reality, were very simple and forthright. Most of what we know (even the concept of atoms) came from the Greeks and historically was passed on to the Romans, then to the Arabs who passed it on to the Europeans. The Europeans took up the baton and reached for the stars.

It is very difficult for me to shut down WWII in my memories; indeed I resist the impulse. The memories keep coming up, not in currents, but like static electricity that bounces here and there. WWII not only is an hour in history, but it rises like Mt. McKinley from the level plain and nothing before or after will ever equal it. WWII was a defining episode in history: it was the culminating worldwide evolution of peoples, movements, cultural conflicts and socio-economics. The participants were also giants. The Germans and the Japanese had giant generals: we are fortunate that the dictators ("Corporal Hitler" as the Brits called him) were so evil they lost their intelligence and were willing to sacrifice the Germans and the world to remain in power. This should not surprise my readers who are acquainted with Evil Incarnate in the world. Then there are the giants on our side - Churchill, Eisenhower, Montgomery, et al.

In our day we have the greatest military of all time. They are volunteers well equipped and well trained. They are superior in many respects to the WWII soldiers. I maintain contact with the present military, correspond with them, watch the Navy Blue Angels fly. I also maintain contact with the old guys who were not so professional but just "sharecroppers" like me who managed to get the job done. They are imprinted in my memory. I am a proud associate member of the Eighth Air Force, the "Mighty Eighth," a card-carrying member of Ancient Aviators of South Alabama and a worshipper of all, men and women, who quieted down the tyrants of WWII.

I am a personal friend of those who bombed in Europe, stormed the beaches of Utah and Omaha, and the 101st Airborne who "straightened out" the Bulge in the Ardennes Forest. Even now and much later in life, my memories come back to those events of 1945. I had a longtime friend (C. N.) in Athens, Alabama. One day we were driving to Huntsville and I casually asked, "C. were you in the war?" I got a nod but not much more. "Why haven't you mentioned it?" "Well, my friend," he replied softly, "I spent my nineteenth birthday crossing the bridge at Remagen on the way to Nuremberg." He further explained that he had seen the dead and frozen from Bastogne to the Rhine and only that year had the overshoes been issued which saved a lot of feet not already frostbitten.

"I seen my duty and I done it" was the countryman's plain analysis of what transpired. There are other accounts of the war but read attorney Jerry Barksdale's "When Duty Calls," the stories of Limestone County, Alabama's soldiers and their families. I have not followed Jerry's marvelous anecdotal style, yet from the local, cultural phenomena we complement one another. Moving to Franklin Springs and experiencing World War II differed almost antipodally from the Depression experience. Truly in history the eras are bound together with hooks, splices and weaves. To me the beginning of WWII was a rebirth, another life. Even before the draft, young men were leaving our community to enlist in the Armed Forces because they knew it was "now or never" for democracy and freedom. Grady Oliver, from a large and poor family, had already started college. J. K. told me that Grady did not even have a coat yet he walked in the cold to the little junior college every day. After Pearl Harbor he joined the Air Force, did not qualify as a pilot because of his eyes, yet as a navigator flew over thirty missions over Germany. Of course, I didn't know about the lack of a coat but I remember his going to war.

Then there was Bern Bennett whose house was on Hwy. 29 near the school bus stop. He was a likeable young man who showed a lot of respect for us smaller people. At Royston High School he was popular and played football for the Purple and White. I can see him now receiving the football in the backfield and making an end sweep to the left. No chinstraps in those days and by the time he reached the line of scrimmage, his helmet had already popped off and he was gaining speed like a train, his blond hair blowing in the breeze he created. If tackled, he would hustle back to the huddle, a teammate would return his helmet and he put it on with a grin, ready for another run.

Bern joined the Navy and soon we heard the news. He was in the observation mast (Crow's Nest) and was shot by a Japanese Zero attack. I just bet he didn't have a helmet. I watched as his father walked the roads in sorrow and spent time on the front porch, rocking back and forth. Bern's Navy buddy came to Franklin Springs and married Bern's sweetheart.

Indirectly, we were close to the war through sports. Ted Williams, the great Red Sox slugger went into the Air Force and returned to play. I had the pleasure of watching him play in Washington, D. C. after the war. We were on a High School Senior Trip, having raised the money by picking cotton, selling magazines and odd jobs in the area. Our bus driver was an avid baseball fan and took several of us baseball fanatics to see the Sox play the Senators. Ted Williams wiggled his right leg and with that marvelous fluid swing of his lifted a homerun into the right field bleachers. What a swing!

We fanatics also followed University of Georgia Football. The University of Georgia was thirty miles away and liked to recruit coal miners' (sorta like sharecroppers) kids from Pennsylvania. When the War got going, two running backs, Frankie Sinkwicz and Charlie Trippi were enrolled at Georgia wearing the red and black. Frankie ploughed straight through the tackles and Charlie sliced left or right, and when he got through the secondary, nobody was going to catch him. Charlie could also throw the pass and was what they called a Triple Threat (throw, run, catch). Both left school for the military and both returned but only Charlie Trippi continued his football career. Frankie Sinkwicz injured a leg or worse, and was unable to continue his career. After the war, we (the Future Farmers of America class) followed Trippi's career each year. Our "Ag" teacher, Coach Newell, took us to watch Trippi play baseball at Ag Hill on the campus. Coach Newell also taught us a lot about baseball in Ty Cobb's hometown.

Yes, in 1942, at ten years of age I had become part of the homeland defense. Six years prior to 1942 I was reading "Nip and Tuck," learning manners in what to say to be excused, to be pardoned if I accidentally stepped on someone's toes, or to be sorry for using an inappropriate word. As I recall I did well with "Nip and Tuck" but not so well matching offense and apology. Papa, who could not go fight the Kaiser and now, too advanced in age to fight against the Nazis, joined the home guard so that if indeed the Germans crossed the Savannah River, he would be ready for them. Each week we went to Royston High School for standing, kneeling and prone rifle practice. I was a fair marksman; Papa was good. But there was a Strickland youngster there not in the military for health reasons, who was stacking his bullets very close together on the target. There was also an older gentleman, who had served in WWI and sported an old Mauser or the like and when he kneeled to shoot, one humorist remarked, "Look out Canon!" Canon was several miles distant.

There was a lot of maturation to be gained while keeping up with the War and *by* keeping up with the War. We left off playing Cowboys and Indians and the *ersatz* was Americans vs. Germans and Japanese. We knew some arithmetic and science but we knew little about physics and nada about nuclear physics. The Manhattan project was a secret but to us it would've still been a secret if we had known about it. We studied something about propulsion but mainly how many grains in a .22 bullet or a 12-gauge shotgun shell. Some of the older guys were firing toy rockets near the printing house, but I swear I didn't know about the fuel being used. Maybe it was benzene. Therefore, we were awed into silence by news of the atomic bomb. We had heard thunder and experienced lightning. In fact, one of my classmates' fathers had been struck and killed by lightning.

We, nor the world, had any concept of nuclear fission and the genius that brought it into reality. We had not yet read *Prometheus Bound* or "The Fire Unleashed." All we knew was that the War in the Pacific would not last long and we felt triumphant. I had already done as much agonizing as Eisenhower did before the invasion of Normandy. The newsreels at the Royston movie finally let us in on the invasion and the terrible costs but somehow we youngsters felt that victory would come although we had a bucketful of doubts. Helpful to us were Principal D.'s special classes he offered to the fifth and sixth graders during the middle of the war and since then I have never been reluctant to talk geography and politics to youngsters. Once they get the image of the compass, the globe and events in focus, children can comprehend a lot, especially if relatives and friends are there in the conflict. Principal D. knew what he was doing: He just had the patience and energy to help us mature and participate.

My children, you are now beginning to understand that ACT I of my life was the Depression, ACT II, The War and I may not reach ACT III, POST-WAR, except by oblique references which support ACTS I and II. All the ACTS are organically connected, yet have individual profiles and separate identities. For certainly after The War, my parents, Ty Cobb and my siblings continued. So did other "wars" and other crises but nothing as awesome as The War. As I've said before, language was the last trait to develop and that's the reason we say, "You know what I mean." For this reason I ask you to read the history of the 1900s to include the Eras I've poorly represented so that with the cues I've dropped, you may become more informed about it. History will repeat itself "because no one was listening the first time it spoke", and again I repeat the immortal words of Heinrich Heine, the Jewish German, "The one thing we learn from history is that *we don't learn from history*."

I can't wait to develop the Eras following The War, namely, the Immediate Post-war, the Korean War, the Eisenhower Years, flagrant Consumerism, Vietnam, Hippies, Yuppies, etc. from a Sharecropper's perspective. My attempt has not been to re-write history but to give a boy's perspective to it: I hope I have been perspicacious as well! "Thank God, I'm a country boy!" sang John Denver. There's a companionship with nature in the country. Every season and human event is in slow motion like an instant replay. We were not overwhelmed with ceaseless and various activities, so we had command of the process. We were in command of our thoughts: we were the captains of our minds. We had no money so we were not continually targeted as a market.

In The War we were all together. Once we had decided against isolation in the conflict, the protests against the war ended. The media and Hollywood began a quasi propaganda to rally support. Several actors joined the armed services. Many, not able to serve, starred in films to stimulate people power. Children, youth, adults and the aged were united. We were watchdogs for, not attack dogs against, our government. Of course, there was a modicum of fraud and exploitation but never so much as in later times. Occasionally, scheming women married several soldiers so they could be the beneficiaries in the event of the soldiers' death but thankfully this was not pervasive. I was utterly horrified to hear of the practice.

As I write my memories of The War, I am reminded of how many died that I might live, and how many lived on and returned to productive lives so that even now we live more abundantly. I hear that in Russia it is popular and in some cases mandated that young couples getting married should have part of the ceremony at the city or town memorial to the fallen heroes who saved the Russian people. Where do American couples marry today? Quite often they marry in church or civil offices, yet very often in some bizarre place or posture. Consider the following marriage sites:

Skydiving; ScubaDiving; At WalMart; Top of the Ferris Wheel; Roller Coasters; En Masse in Las Vegas On Morning Television Shows;

We should drag their culos out to the cemeteries for part of the ceremony. The nation not honoring its dead has no respect for itself.

Sometimes a single event may change our lives as in the case of Ty Cobb. He had worked so hard to be a success at baseball because his father had required success. But at the very time he broke into major league ball, his father was killed. Ty believed that his father was still watching so he played with vigor until he was the best. He was honoring the deceased.

About the same year that Hershel Cobb was killed (c. 1905), Papa's father died. Papa, the eldest, set his face and career to raise up the siblings, as contrary as a couple of my uncles were! Why? Papa honored the deceased.

Consider The War as one continuous event, one overwhelming image, one four-year composite. Millions paid the price, hundreds of thousands made the supreme sacrifice. I look upon The War as a great synthesis of the past and a format for the future. 1939 was TEOTWAWKI and 1946 was TBOTWAWKI (The Beginning...), or perhaps The End of the Beginning and the Beginning of the End. The End came in 1939 and the Next End is up the road.

Beginning/End, Beginning/End... everything except Infinity has two sides.

Hitler is dead. The Russians kept it a secret for a long time. Many in the West thought he had escaped. Hitler was a unique dictator in that he was supported by a modern, scientific, and capable nation. It was evident that others would pop up around the world when attention was being focused on the ideological and geographical confrontations between Titan U. S. /Britain and Titan Soviets/Stalin. The future was partially clear at the meetings of the Titans at Yalta and Tehran. Even before the end of The War, the coming Cold War showed its colors.

When time permits I shall give the old Sharecropper's perspective on the "little dog dictators" who emerged when the Big Dogs were dickering for hegemony in Europe. Fortunately the Big Dogs knew what the outcome of a fight would be: the Little Dogs had no idea what would happen to them if the Big Dogs decided to put them down. The partitioning of Germany was another example of winning the war and losing the peace. War is permanent, peace is temporary; poverty is permanent, plenty is temporary. Draw your own analogies on the subject and you'll find that most of your expectations have only temporary fulfillments. I don't know when we developed a policy of killing the people and saving the dictator. If we are going to be drawn into war anyway due to duty or national interests, then we need to form a policy of benevolent aggression. People who need help must let the helper have free rein, otherwise don't call.

THE END OF THE BEGINNING: 1945

Which Greek philosophers advised, "Either marry well or become a philosopher?" The shortcut to philosophy is to be born into a sharecropper's family. Apart from the "can to can't" workday (light to dark), we never had to work overtime to pay for laborsaving devices such as appliances and gimmicks. Becoming a philosopher also depends on the personality that comes with birth. A sharecropper must not desire "a better life" because he has all of the advantages already, viz. the untrammeled life I just mentioned and all the material things he doesn't have to worry about being lost or depleted. He can put all his goods and belongings into a 2-horse wagon. The only people luckier I know about are the horizontal (rangers) and vertical (valley to mountains) nomads of the desert fringes and steppes of the world, who can break camp and move in minutes.

Henry Thesiger, the great British explorer, wished to cross the formidable Rubh Al'Khali (the Empty Quarter) of Saudi Arabia. The authorities in Southern Arabia recommended a guide. He was summoned, and appeared in the doorway, a thin, sparse man in traditional Bedouin dress (literally): Sandals, *Kofiah* (Headdress), a sash about the waist holding dry dates and a small goatskin bag of water. Over his shoulder swung an ancient rifle and a cartridge belt.

They exchanged greetings and formalities and

agreed on the venture. "When can you be ready to travel?" queried Thesiger. "Now" replied the Bedouin without any change in his voice rhythm. I wish to tell the reader that the guide brought Thesiger to the Northern side of the Empty Quarter while saving his life several times.

My younger sister (the "kid," the "gypsy") was a more natural philosopher than I was but I compensated by studying philosophy (metaphysics) in college. She was on the sidelines more than I. Undernourished, she had to spend more time thinking than physically exercising. Even today we go back in mind to the 30s and 40s to reevaluate our beginnings and to see how they played out when we left sharecropping to join the greater world. We did survive in the microscopic world of sharecropping and our flourishing was in this business of philosophy. The genius of it all was that my memories started earlier but she remained at home after I entered the greater world. We had comparable insights into the world beyond the horizon in 1942 when Second Son and our sister-in-law came to help with the planting and cultivation prior to his joining the Navy. His wife was from New Orleans and had an acquaintance with the big city and the culture beyond our pale. With good vocabulary and infinite patience, she discussed subjects quite apart from materialism and movies. This intelligent introduction to the outside world made it possible for us to peel off the husks and get to the grain. I hope she realized how much contribution she made in our lives.

Royston had a small public library during the war. The street just east of the main square cornered at Blumenthal's Dry Goods and halfway south down the block, there was an entrance and stairs went up to the Library. I went up those stairs at every opportunity to talk to the librarian and to discuss her recommended reading. She discouraged my getting into a genre rut and talked me into reading a variety of subjects and encouraged me to analyze content and style. She and my public school teachers quietly but firmly improved my vision, analytical powers, vocabulary and grammatical usage. One just never knows how much influence they have in the lives of these country youngsters who would otherwise be wasting our precious free time on materialism. So I kept checking out the books and walking 2 1/2 miles back to Franklin Springs.

On the other side of this square was a dental office newly set up by a Navy doctor just coming in from military rotation. He was a great person, but had basically torture equipment and I had several molar cavities. Papa let me walk into town in the winter months and I did some duties at the 5 & 10 store nearby. I used all my money to pay the dentist but I still have my teeth. Now you say, "How did this improve your philosophy?" Well, I'll tell you… I, as a youngster, dreaded to walk up those steps as much as I enjoyed the other steps to the Library. I learned that one must overcome dread to take the road leading to progress and improvement. We sharecroppers learned to make personal sacrifices to do what is right. The great philosopher Immanuel Kant (whom I've mentioned) was rather naive in his estimate of human nature, yet he concluded correctly that yet if one will actually "will to do good" he had made an excellent decision.

I see people today enslaved by nicotine, amphetamines, barbiturates, cocaine and alcohol. We learned in the early years that a lack of will is a loss of freedom. Truly in the Depression and The War we saw a lot of life objectively. "Silence is wisdom and listening is learning." It's not impossible but it's very difficult, to learn with you mouth open. As I told you, we used to kid one another, "Heh! As an outsider what do you think of the human race?" Being an outsider does not mean being eccentric, strange or pathological. One can learn more by watching the parade than by marching in the parade. You know that one of the greatest descriptions of people is by Geoffrey Chaucer as he sat in a corner at Tabard Inn watching the pilgrims assembling for Canterbury. In a thousand words he drew pictures of a dozen or more pilgrims. One of my former students, B. A. sketched portraits from these words to hang on the walls of my literature class. Chaucer's *Tales* came alive as we read this marvelous work.

The Chinese say, "Too soon old, too late smart." In the days of Kung Fu (Confucius) and Lao Tsu, there was more time and disposition toward reflection. In friendly debate with my Democrat friends I would tease "Confucius was a Democrat because he proposed 'Give a person beans and rice, he will be good,' whereas Lao Tsu, the Republican, retorted 'If a person is good, he will grow his own beans and rice!' Therefore I'm a Republican!"

My kinship with Kung Fu began very early when I discovered that he took common youths into his academy and taught them dignity, respect, practical philosophy and purpose. His students anticipated a time when they could become humble, competent rulers of a decadent society. Unfortunately in our day the "Money" politicians emerge as winners. Only occasionally does an "Abraham Lincoln" step down from the stump to assume leadership. Would that we had grasped more fully the confidence that our Royston teachers had in us. It is very difficult for a sharecropper to imagine the universal role that he should play in the greater society. After The War, I went out in that society and accomplished a little; Third Son came back to the sharecropper environment and with great sacrifice brightened his corner of the world. More often in the greater world we get caught in the riptide and we lose the balance of our simple beginnings. We compromise values for vogues.

"Mr. Smith" went to Washington and did not compromise his provincial values. All too often, elected officials go to Washington but drink too much Potomac water, get Potomac fever and lose the disciplined values they gained on the farm to avoid being profiled by the media as bumpkins and rustics. Presidents like Jimmy Carter are mauled by the old "sophisticates" who lie in wait to trap and discredit these countrymen who eventually attempt to "conform" to another image and end in failure. Therefore it is not surprising that many potential leaders do not wish to be barbecued in Washington in the interest of aiding the Country. We actually need to move the Capitol to St. Louis, Kansas City or Oklahoma City. Since Ancient times capitols have been moved to the benefit of the Nation. Land travel is becoming more necessary and popular and we may be able to make even California feel like part of the U. S. A. if we move the Capitol to Kansas City or such. Even if the move doesn't help "it won't ho'it" as Jewish Vaudeville says it.

In retrospect I often think that 1946 should've been frozen in time. Men and women were coming home (Yankee, Come home!) from around the world. There was joy, tranquility, a calm (unfortunately before the Storm of Consumerism, Capitalism and more war) and an aura never to be forgotten. We were a population regretting the loss of life but vowing to keep the peace. The same population knew its power of accomplishment. Consumer goods were emerging but we had learned how little we needed (and wanted) and how much we could disdain. We had found contentment by hitherto unimaginable media. The carpetbaggers of consumerism had not yet arrived to change our philosophy. The supply side had not created demand.

In 1946, demand and supply were in harmony in the sharecropper world. In 1926, *Harper's Magazine* printed a brilliant expose of the cruelty of supply's creating the demand in "The Confessions of a Former Ford Dealer" in which the methods of supply bombarded a moral, upright Ford dealer until he went out of business.

My grandchildren, I found many essays in my youth, which are available to you now. You can live a hundred years without them but never so well. "The Confessions of a Former Ford Dealer" (by Sprague?); "Bleak House" by Dickens, especially "Jarndyce vs. Jarndyce" (every lawyer and judge should read it); The Nature of the Universe by Lucretius; and the list goes on. By college age I had debated many subjects and in many cases the original philosophy may be my own.

For forty years I have debated the so-called "Bill of Rights" so superbly written by James Madison, all four feet, eleven inches of him. About thirty years ago I described the Bill of Rights as a Trojan Horse, a Sacred Cow and an Albatross. The British left us the Horse, we converted it to a Cow and now wear it about our necks as an Albatross. Very definitely the Bill was a demand by the yeomen of our country who had lived under British occupation. They did not realize that the British had gone forever. Living with the Albatross we have allowed the criminal elements and political perverts to sabotage our liberties with the bleats of "freedom." One day some bright attorney from a reputable law school will see the light and blurt out "The Bill of Rights is an anachronism!" Then all the stooges, media, etc. will echo "What a novelty? Why hasn't anyone thought of this before?"

Everyone knows about the Bill of Rights but no one really reads it. ("Classic: A book which people praise and don't read." - Mark Twain). Read it and you'll realize that the liberated colonials do not feel liberated. They think the British are still there. There was an elephant on a 25 ft. chain for 25 years. Then they took the chain off and the elephant would only move about within a 25 ft. radius. Maybe it's too late to remove the chains! Anyway, check out editorials by me in the *Huntsville Times* (Alabama) from about twenty-five years ago.

There we were in 1946... Only nine of us siblings remained. Nine of the twelve yet lived with Mama and Papa, therefore, in the count we were still eleven in number. Some of the older siblings had already experienced the world, First Son in the Civilian Conservation Corp in the North Georgia mountains where the sun arose at 10:00 A.M. and set at 4:00 in the afternoon, and in the oil fields of Texas where the sun lasted all day, and Second Son in Atlanta and Mobile with a mapping co. Then the girls began their sojourns. First and Second of the daughters took advantage of the National Youth Administration (NYA) programs and enrolled in a program at Toccoa Falls College in North Georgia in the late '30s.

There had been a migration (transhumance, as sociologists say) of people from South to North in the late 30s and early 40s. Yet in my world, Atlanta was still the sharecropper's window on the universe. Daughter number Three went to Atlanta in 1946 after serving as a elementary school teacher two years at Gumlog (near Lavonia, Georgia and heralded as the "Moonshine Capital of the World"). She enjoyed teaching yet transportation and lodging were awkward so she opted for more regulated living. So guess her first stop in Atlanta... You're right! Sears, Roebuck and Company on Ponce de Leon Avenue, almost immediately across from the Atlanta Cracker's Stadium of the old Southern League. A great number of athletes were returning from the War and baseball resumed in earnest.

Destiny was to change Atlanta from a great, traditional, historical small city where one could meet fellow croppers and tenants at the corner of Forsyth and Alabama or at Ponce de Leon and Peachtree at the Fox Theatre every day. Sears was the big siphon, which drew croppers in and then distributed them to other opportunities in the City. Since General Sherman's "Urban Renewal Plan", the city had grown slowly and wisely and whereas the big cities of the North received hundreds of thousands from the South, the newcomers seldom felt at home but Atlanta was our city, our pride, our destiny in 1946 and we never entertained the idea of mutation, metamorphosis or identity loss. Ben Johnson would have said "He who tires of Atlanta tires of life."

Dream on, ye who would freeze 1946 in time. It was just a calm before the storm yet the wiser ones enjoyed the year without the dread of the inevitable. "Gather ye rosebuds while ye may," "Work for the night is coming," "Sufficient unto the day is the evil thereof," "Ninety percent of our fears never transpire"... and the list goes on. At Royston High I loved 1946. My brother was at home and I could hardly wait to get home, change into work clothes and hunt him down whether he was at the barn, in the fields or the woods. Counter-point to the Crash of '29 was the basking tranquility and inner strength of 1946. The job abroad was finished (so we thought) and the job at home was stabilized (so we hoped).

In 1946 I was faced with departing from my window on the world as a spectator to entering the world at large as a participant. Who am I, and what's out there? To what degree shall I be a conformist or a revolutionary? As a sharecropper's son, I had always felt that the world belonged to someone else. I saw Brothers Two and Three return from the War virtually unaffected by the military and geographical experience. They simply wished to return to their ingrained lifestyle and pursuits.

I eventually was to learn that there is no particular culture in the world one must adopt or adapt to without being eccentric, rebellious or revolutionary. But how was I to know this in 1946 with such limited data from the outside world? Many of my contemporaries who did not have the sharecropper experience had already locked into a modicum of achievement and external experience. I could already see their vision of participating in the family business, working in the limited local business, journeying to Atlanta or the military, or even going on to college. I was to discover that a modicum of success in high school might become satisfying and youth could become static in such a posture; however, the opposite might spur the "non-achiever" on to greater (though no more noble) accomplishments.

After 1946 I spent two more years in Royston High, graduated in the upper twenty percent of the class at the advanced age of sixteen years. I shall try to describe the years following 1946 in a subsequent memory picking called "A Sharecropper's Son Leaves Home." I followed the Pied Piper initially but in time followed my own music and directed my own course (hoed and picked my own cotton row).

After going to press with these memories, I shall recall (since the pent-up memories are beginning to seep out) more thoughts and experiences from the 1934-1946 Era, and moreover septua-octo-and novegenerians reading my inadequate words may recall more trenchant and vivid memories from that Era. If so, I hope they will write these down and relay them to me. I shall print them in a Preamble to the next Era.

End

POSTSCRIPTS

I assigned a term paper when I taught in college. Some of my students perceived the assignment to be "Busywork" and suspected that I would never read the papers. One of my students, after several pages, wrote "Dear Professor, if you've read this far I'll buy you dinner at the place of your choice." I returned their papers several days later and for about another week observed the expressions on the student's face. When convinced that he was beginning to feel triumphant, I paused in my lecture and queried "Douglas, when are you going to buy me dinner?" His jaw dropped in astonishment.

So... if some of my descendants have read this far, I have a few more experiences to offer. I remember being very comfortable at home on the farm with my parents and siblings, yet away from home I was mostly timid and quiescent. My occasional outbursts of aggression and daring did not serve me well especially since my growth was delayed by undernourishment and my social standing by lack of graces. I do not accept this state of mind as entirely my persona but attribute it also to the sharecropper's experience. There was a different world beyond the confines of the landlord's property that I had to deal with and from retrospect I urge my grandchildren and great-grandchildren to attain great solidarity at home and walk circumspectly beyond the pale of their home and culture. Do a lot of listening and philosophical digestion and learn from other people's experiences. "Experience may be the best teacher" but you do not have to learn only from your own. If you see the runners up ahead disappearing over a cliff or a bridge-out, stop running. You don't need the experience. As I've told my grandson many times, "Don't take a dare." If someone dares you to do a dangerous act, say "You do it: it's your idea."

When we lived at Franklin Springs, we were always "the folks on the creek." The creek also received the sewage effluent from the original Emmanuel College School and dormitory. I don't know how we managed to remain clear of illness and disease from that experience of living downstream. And, further downstream from us the city dumped septic tank cleanings into the stream. Nevertheless, the President of the College was a fine gentleman and our relationship was very good. He loved to hunt quail and dove and had two fine pointer dogs. It occurred to him that it would be good if could pen his dogs on the farm and I could feed and water them. Food should be no problem because daily I could go to the college cafeteria and get scraps (commercial dog food was unknown in those days) for the dogs. The plan seemed ideal but the execution of the same was more traumatic.

I remember appearing for the first time at the kitchen door for my bucket of scraps. A burly cook, wiping his hands on his apron turned and confronted me with "wot yo' want, boy?" Well, these were new words for me and they sounded hostile. I timidly explained my mission and he reluctantly and flippantly began to fling scraps of burnt toast and such into the bucket. I should've brought Papa on the first trip to establish the mandate but I didn't. I dreaded returning but I did return and had to listen to the same litany, which had not changed in tone or substance.

Well, the dogs didn't like the scraps and began to get thin. My sharecropper dog was more culturally enlightened and ate them with enthusiasm. Moreover, I hated to pen dogs in such an undesirable state so I would open the gate and let them run. What I did not know was that bird dogs never stop. They run in squares, circles, quadrilaterals and triangles but do not stop. They became thin as clotheslines and I could not prevent the slide. O that I could explain the malevolence of the cooks at the college yet the sharecropper experience kept me from self-vindication.

Eventually the President came to the creek to hunt with his dogs and I'll never forget the disappointed look on his face and I just accepted the blame quietly. We sharecroppers weren't part of the "Blame Generation." Well, the President has gone to his reward now (may his memory be blessed) and I have my reward, too. The cooks have now gone to their reward and my calculation is that their reward is a bit less than the President's.

In my next book I shall relate my encounter with the Toccoa Falls College cooks when it was my duty to pick up Sunday lunch for the President's home. I still resented the "wot yo' want, boy?" but I considered the cooks' professional milieu more and had outgrown some of my timidity and remained calm. One of their comments was "Whar yo' from, boy? I bet you're from one of those 'springs' places." He was right on target because I was from the "Springs." Being a scholar I studied the development of the Piedmont initially around "springs" and then the Piedmonters began to dig wells. What the cooks intended as a pejorative I capitalized on conceptually. My children, when you get a lemon...!

If you're still listening and still young, you may wish to think about your unique situation. Preferably you are poor with decent parents. If poor with uncaring parents, your task will be more difficult but the rewards will be greater. You must claim divine providence that you find yourself in such a circumstance. You will perceive your sibling as part of the divine quadrant because truly you are a unique being. You should seek to sit at the feet of positive, compassionate elderly people who acquaint you with the Wisdom of Solomon. I remember the house whose high front porch overlooked the pavilion at Franklin Springs. Each Sunday afternoon two of my older contemporaries would pull up their chairs and sit by the rocker of the venerable old gentleman. I observed the behavior of the two young men and noticed their daily attitudes and behavior, which seemed elicited by this relationship.

For you older youth I urge you to befriend a skinny undernourished youngster who may unselfishly make a difference in the world simply because someone cared. Moreover, to the skinny kid I recommend finding a way to learn and succeed. Of course I had some of the right cultivation from the Third Son from the Rock yet the self-esteem and "carpe diem" I gained from him led me to collect post-season bird nests and classify them with the North Georgia birds. I had the further advantage of living with nature, identifying flora and fauna by my own system. I wondered how buckwheat and soybeans could add protein to my diet, and did my best without success to swim upstream in Broad River where the river channeled and sped up around a bar.

First, I think you will have an advantage in being disadvantaged. You should be able to find an area to excel outside of fads and popularity. Even beyond the lap of nature you should be able to find a hobby and avocation suitable for your personal and cultural growth. In addition you're not too young to discover universal laws of physics and metaphysics that will propel you beyond the frivolous and commonplace. Remember the "Bird Man of Alcatraz?" My kid sister and I used to discuss ideas far beyond our local environs.

In my youth, in comparative isolation, I had to get acquainted with myself. What I gained in woods, fields and the blessed hayloft on rainy days is incalculable. The self is the most difficult subject to learn so get busy. You must keep in mind that "Everything is connected to everything else" and that you are a part of the universe, categorically and individually.

Becoming comfortably established in the third grade at Royston, I became less timid but I was also to learn propriety. After recess one day in the fourth grade, I returned to the room brimming with enthusiasm and loudly proclaiming my thoughts. I learned immediately that recess ended before one entered the classroom. Ms. Ginn simply turned me around and sent me back through the doorway. I spent most of the next class period outside, embarrassed by every passer-by. After becoming an instructor, I remember that the current generation chatters five minutes after entering class and would chatter the whole period if not admonished to be quiet and even then they are very anxious to tell all they know. They have not learned to whisper, a device that lends to credibility! People are interested in what others are whispering and gesturing. Talking simply gets louder and louder. Who said, "Silence is wisdom – Listening is learning."

I have often thought about my fourth-grade experience and it had served me well over the years. Be quiet and studious and people will think you're smart. Besides, it is difficult to learn with your mouth open even though occasionally ones ears may hear what ones mouth is saying.

You must regard every event as a divine happening whether brushing your teeth or finding a book on Greek mythology. Moreover, refrain from spoon-fed audio-visuals, TV etc. The alphabet and reading were divine revelations and they induce imagination and reward. The creation of images and scenarios in the mind stimulates consciousness of an exciting reality. When I was ten years of age, Chaucer, Zane Grey and J. Fenimore Cooper were creating people and nature, personalities and landscapes for me as I transcended time and space from my sharecropper milieu. The great writers stimulated, inspired and launched me from the Commonplace. This is education. Ben Gurion of Israel aspired for everyone, including street sweepers, to have an education. Hence, the most common people can converse with you about history.

Occasionally, as a youngster, I used to share my transcendence with Avery Cromer and he never betrayed me: I occasionally shared something with T. B., C. R. or C. G. and they would embarrass me in front of their friends. This only happened once per traitor. I learned to stick with Avery and my kid sister. Therefore, my children, look beyond the pop culture to transcend to universal values. You remember the Greek story of the Titan Prometheus ("FORETHOUGHT') who had compassion on mankind because mankind did not have fire to cook food and to warm himself, nor did he harness the ox to the plough and the sail to the boat. The story goes that Prometheus stole the secrets (metallurgy, animal power, fire and its potential) of the Gods and gave them to man. Zeus was so angry that he commanded his servants to chain Prometheus to a rock so the vultures could come and pick at his liver. The sharecropper's youngster thought that this was an unconscionable and unforgivable act but in time he began to wonder. Truly, the command to tie Prometheus came from Zeus' pride and anger yet the consequences of Prometheus' treachery began to make man's life softer, took away man's strength and will to survive, eventually provided man with the knowledge to build nuclear weapons ("unleashed the fire") and a number of inventions which are impressive yet questionable as good for mankind. Prometheus' act tricked mankind into increasing beyond his ability to feed himself and to make war to gain political and economic power. Go figure! Truly man was not moral enough to handle what he had "wrought." Man has dislodged things (neutral in themselves) from the earth and has formulated dangerous mixes of chemicals and minerals.

Fortunately, at Royston we had access to literature but lamentably chemistry and the physical sciences were not available. Still, literature helps us to think and thinking helps us to grow. Books, to Abraham Lincoln and to us sharecroppers are the keys to the universe. From books we build mental images and accept the challenge of interpretation and classifying the minutiae written for us. Television (even with all the documentaries) does the thinking and analysis for us and deprives us of autonomy. I suspect that future generations will have mutated into robots and physically will have eyes the size of baseballs from viewing television and heads the size of golf balls from not thinking. "If you don't use it, you'll lose it" and "if you can have it and not know it, you can lose it and not miss it."

It may be that the generation who reads this humble book will be affluent and culturally deprived of the sharecropper experience. Yet perchance there will be some from large, poor families (or for that matter, small, poor families) and they will see the advantage of being themselves and of taking advantage of every opportunity which presents itself.

Some thoughts from the Holy Scriptures and other sources will loom large:

1.) "I have learned to be content, regardless of the condition in which I find myself."
2.) "Whatsoever thy hand findest to do, do it with all thy might."
3.) Moses found himself, a fugitive in the desert. He told God that he had no weapons or devices. God said "What is that in your hand?" It was a shepherd's staff and he used it to liberate his people. (What is in your hand or at hand?)
4.) George Washington Carver affirmed that a thousand mile journey begins with a single step.
5.) St. Paul proposed that we "Run the race that is set before you." Don't wait for the ideal race. Run!

In retrospect I have the opinion that I was poorer economically and materially than anyone in my class during the Depression and World War II. I had nothing to lose and everything to gain. Fortunately I did not strive for material gains. Some mysterious force instilled in me the desire to learn about geography, history and literature. The foregoing is not boasting but is described so that some little person, accessing my book, may be challenged toward mundial knowledge and wisdom for their own sake. Remember "Sir Edmund, why did you climb Mt. Everest?" "Because it was there" was the reply.

For you older readers, give attention to those little ones, especially the poor, about you. Encourage their dreams and direct them to pursue their abilities. In a democracy the little ones may mature into statesmen, writers, scientists, philanthropists and the roster is endless. Remember the words of the Galilean "Whoever abuses one of these little ones, 'tis better for him to have a millstone hanged about his neck and be thrown into the sea." A little boy north of the Sea of Galilee gave his lunch to Jesus, and Jesus fed a whole multitude of people. Who's to say that poor little boys and girls will not grow up to serve the multitudes?

"Again folks, goodbye for now. Send me your stories about the Great Depression and WWII."

Bert Hayes
P. O. Box 6300
Gulf Shores, Alabama 36547

3 כָּרַת עִמָּנוּ בְּרִית בְּחֹרֵב: לֹא אֶת־אֲבֹתֵינוּ כָּרַת יְהוָֹה
אֶת־הַבְּרִית הַזֹּאת כִּי אִתָּנוּ אֲנַחְנוּ אֵלֶּה פֹה הַיּוֹם כֻּלָּנוּ

4 חַיִּים: פָּנִים ׀ בְּפָנִים דִּבֶּר יְהוָה עִמָּכֶם בָּהָר מִתּוֹךְ

ה הָאֵשׁ: אָנֹכִי עֹמֵד בֵּין־יְהוָה וּבֵינֵיכֶם בָּעֵת הַהִוא לְהַגִּיד
לָכֶם אֶת־דְּבַר יְהוָה כִּי יְרֵאתֶם מִפְּנֵי הָאֵשׁ וְלֹא־עֲלִיתֶם

6 בָּהָר לֵאמֹר: ס אָנֹכִי יְהוָה אֱלֹהֶיךָ אֲשֶׁר הוֹצֵאתִיךָ

7 מֵאֶרֶץ מִצְרַיִם מִבֵּית עֲבָדִים: לֹא־יִהְיֶה לְךָ אֱלֹהִים

8 אֲחֵרִים עַל־פָּנָי: לֹא־תַעֲשֶׂה־לְךָ פֶסֶל ׀ כָּל־תְּמוּנָה אֲשֶׁר
בַּשָּׁמַיִם ׀ מִמַּעַל וַאֲשֶׁר בָּאָרֶץ מִתָּחַת וַאֲשֶׁר בַּמַּיִם ׀

9 מִתַּחַת לָאָרֶץ: לֹא־תִשְׁתַּחֲוֶה לָהֶם וְלֹא תָעָבְדֵם כִּי אָנֹכִי
יְהוָה אֱלֹהֶיךָ אֵל קַנָּא פֹּקֵד עֲוֺן אָבֹת עַל־בָּנִים וְעַל־

י שִׁלֵּשִׁים וְעַל־רִבֵּעִים לְשֹׂנְאָי: וְעֹשֶׂה חֶסֶד לַאֲלָפִים
לְאֹהֲבַי וּלְשֹׁמְרֵי מִצְוֺתָו: ס לֹא תִשָּׂא אֶת־שֵׁם־יְהוָה

11 אֱלֹהֶיךָ לַשָּׁוְא כִּי לֹא יְנַקֶּה יְהוָה אֵת אֲשֶׁר־יִשָּׂא אֶת־שְׁמוֹ

12 לַשָּׁוְא: ס שָׁמוֹר אֶת־יוֹם הַשַּׁבָּת לְקַדְּשׁוֹ כַּאֲשֶׁר צִוְּךָ ׀
יְהוָה אֱלֹהֶיךָ: שֵׁשֶׁת יָמִים תַּעֲבֹד וְעָשִׂיתָ כָּל־מְלַאכְתֶּךָ:

13

14 וְיוֹם הַשְּׁבִיעִי שַׁבָּת ׀ לַיהוָה אֱלֹהֶיךָ לֹא תַעֲשֶׂה כָל־
מְלָאכָה אַתָּה וּבִנְךָ וּבִתֶּךָ וְעַבְדְּךָ וַאֲמָתֶךָ וְשׁוֹרְךָ וַחֲמֹרְךָ
וְכָל־בְּהֶמְתֶּךָ וְגֵרְךָ אֲשֶׁר בִּשְׁעָרֶיךָ לְמַעַן יָנוּחַ עַבְדְּךָ

טו וַאֲמָתְךָ כָּמוֹךָ: וְזָכַרְתָּ כִּי־עֶבֶד הָיִיתָ ׀ בְּאֶרֶץ מִצְרַיִם
וַיֹּצִאֲךָ יְהוָֹה אֱלֹהֶיךָ מִשָּׁם בְּיָד חֲזָקָה וּבִזְרֹעַ נְטוּיָה עַל־

16 כֵּן צִוְּךָ יְהוָה אֱלֹהֶיךָ לַעֲשׂוֹת אֶת־יוֹם הַשַּׁבָּת: ס כַּבֵּד אֶת־
אָבִיךָ וְאֶת־אִמֶּךָ כַּאֲשֶׁר צִוְּךָ יְהוָה אֱלֹהֶיךָ לְמַעַן ׀ יַאֲרִיכֻן
יָמֶיךָ וּלְמַעַן יִיטַב לָךְ עַל הָאֲדָמָה אֲשֶׁר־יְהוָה אֱלֹהֶיךָ

17 נֹתֵן לָךְ: ס לֹא תִּרְצָח: ס וְלֹא תִּנְאָף: ס וְלֹא

18 תִּגְנֹב: ס וְלֹא־תַעֲנֶה בְרֵעֲךָ עֵד שָׁוְא: ס וְלֹא
תַחְמֹד אֵשֶׁת רֵעֶךָ ס וְלֹא תִתְאַוֶּה בֵּית רֵעֶךָ שָׂדֵהוּ
וְעַבְדּוֹ

Bill of Rights

Amendment I
Congress shall make no law respecting an establishment of religion, or prohibiting the free exercise therof; or abridging the freedom of speech, or of the press; or the right of the people peaceably to assemble, and to petition the government for a redress of grievances.

Amendment II
A well regulated militia, being necessary to the security of a free state, the right of the people to keep and bear arms, shall not be infringed.

Amendment III
No soldier shall, in time of peace be quartered in any house, without the consent of the owner, not in time of war, but in a manner to be prescribed by law.

Amendment IV
The right of the people to be secure in their persons, houses, papers, and effect, against unreasonable searches and seizures, shall not be violated, and no warrants shall issue, but upon probable cause, supported by oath or affirmation, and particularly describing the place to be searched, and the persons or things to be seized.

Amendment V
No person shall be held to answer for a capital, or otherwise infamous crime, unless on a presentment or indictment of a grand jury, except in cases arising in the land or naval forces, or in the militia, when in actual service in time of war or public danger; nor shall any person be subject for the same offense to be twice put in jeopardy of life or limb; nor shall be compelled in any criminal case to be a witness against himself, nor be deprived of life, liberty, or property, without due process of law; nor shall private property be taken for public use, without just compensation.

Amendment VI
In all criminal prosecutions, the accused shall enjoy the right to a speedy and public trial, by an impartial jury of the state and district wherein the crime shall have been committed, which district shall have been previously ascertained by law, and to be informed of the nature and cause of the accusation; to be confronted with the witnesses against him; to have compulsory process for obtaining witnesses in his favor, and to have the assistance of counsel for his defense.

Amendment VII
In suits of common law, where the value in controversy shall exceed twenty dollars, the right of trial by jury shall be preserved, and no fact tried by a jury, shall be otherwise reexamined in any court of the United States, than according to the rules of the common law.

Amendment VIII
Excessive bail shall not be required, nor excessive fines imposed, nor cruel and unusual punishments inflicted.

Amendment IX
The enumeration in the Constitution, of certain rights, shall not be construed to deny or disparage others retained by the people.

Amendment X
The powers not delegated to the United States by the Constitution, nor prohibited by it to the states, are reserved to the states respectively, or to the people.

CURRENT NEW FRANKLIN CHRISTIAN CHURCH WHICH
REPLACED THE WOOD STRUCTURE OF THE
SHARECROPPING ERA NEAR THE GRADY SCHOOL SITE.
FRANKLIN COUNTY, GEORGIA

MASON'S MILL IN THE PIEDMONT WATER SHED. CREEK
AND WATERWHEEL IN THE BACKGROUND. OH, THE
MEMORIES OF MASON'S MILL!
MADISON COUNTY, GEORGIA

ONE HALF OF SHARECROPPER FAMILY (MINUS TWO)
HAYES - OLBON

ONE HALF OF SHARECROPPER FAMILY. OTHER HALF IN THE
FIELD OR IN THE PIPELINE BUILDING.
HAYES - OLBON

ARTIST'S BUILDING MURAL WITH CONCEPT OF ROYSTON'S
BECOMING A RAILROAD TOWN IN THE LATE 1880'S. DISREGARD
MOUNTAINS IN THE BACKGROUND. MOUNTAINS ARE THIRTY
(30) MILES NORTH OF ROYSTON, NOT EAST. WALL MURAL
ON JOE T. CUNNINGHAM BUILDING.
(JOE T. WAS ONE OF TY COBB'S BEST FRIENDS)
FRANKLIN COUNTY, GEORGIA

"WHISTLE STOP" FACING THE OLD SOUTHERN RAILROAD TRACK
IN BOWERSVILLE GEORGIA. DOOR JAMBS HAVE FIGURES
WEARING EASTERN HEAD DRESS.
FRANKLIN COUNTY, GEORGIA

THE KIDS ARE
GROWING AND
SOME ARE GROWN.
LOVE AND A
WINTER'S SUPPLY
OF FIREWOOD
REMAIN.
FRANKLIN COUNTY,
GEORGIA

SQUEEZING CANE STALKS
GENERIC DRAWING

TURNING THE SOD WITH A SINGLE FOOT PLOW
GENERIC DRAWING

LOADING CANE ON SUV
SHARECROPPER UTILITY VEHICLE
GENERIC DRAWING

GRANDKIDS CONCEPT OF MILLHOUSE, RACE AND WHEEL.
EXTERIOR CREEK FLOWS DOWN FROM MILLPOND ABOVE.

PARHAM - HAYES MILL

GRANKIDS CONCEPT OF SYRUP-MAKING BUILDING AT
PARHAM - HAYES MILL

GRANDKIDS CONCEPT OF MILLHOUSE INTERIOR/EXTERIOR
MILLRACE AND WHEEL

PARHAM - HAYES MILL

GRANKIDS CONCEPT OF SUV
SHARECROPPER UTILITY VEHICLE

GRANDKIDS CONCEPT AT SQUEEZING CANE JUICE

GRANKIDS CONCEPT OF TAKING RAW COTTON TO COTTON
ENGINE (GIN)

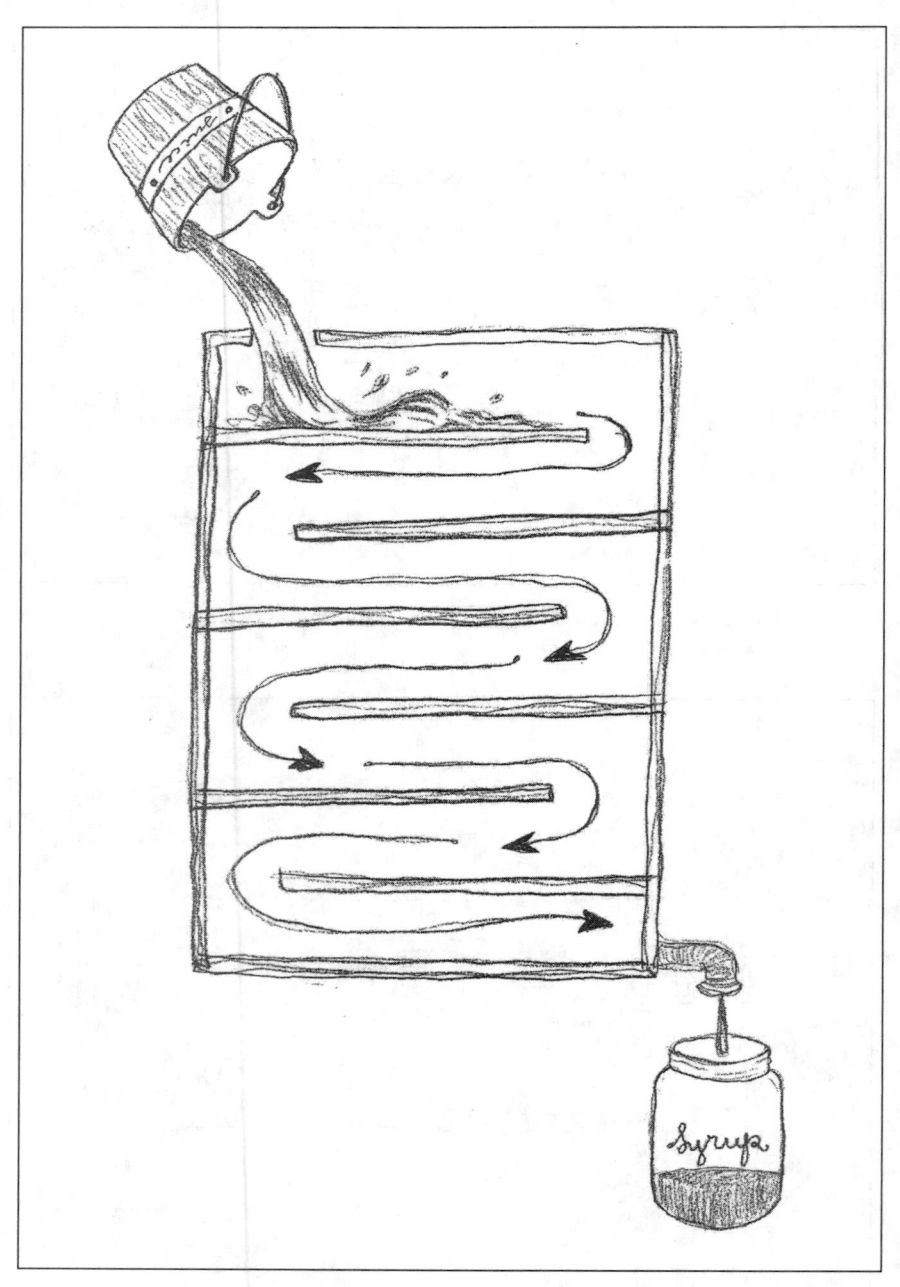

GRANDKIDS CONCEPT OF EVAPORATOR WHICH TURNS
JUICE INTO SYRUP